Baby
Development

Everything you need to know

Baby
Development

Everything you need to know

Dr. Claire Halsey

London • New York • Melbourne • Munich • Delhi

Dedication
This book is dedicated to my mother,
Patricia Higginbotham

Project Editor Claire Cross
US Editor Jane Perlmutter
Designer Hannah Moore
Senior Editor Mandy Lebentz
US Senior Editor Shannon Beatty
Senior Art Editor Sarah Ponder
Managing Editor Penny Warren
Managing Art Editor Glenda Fisher
Production Editor Maria Elia
Production Controller Alice Sykes
Creative Technical Support Sonia Charbonnier
Art Director Lisa Lanzarini
Category Publisher Peggy Vance
Editorial Consultant Karen Sullivan
US Medical Consultant Aviva Schein, MD
Photographer Ruth Jenkinson
Photography Art Direction Peggy Sadler

First American Edition, 2012

Published in the United States by
DK Publishing
375 Hudson Street
New York, New York 10014

12 13 14 15 16   10 9 8 7 6 5 4 3 2 1

001 — 178243 — May/2012

Published in Great Britain by Dorling Kindersley Limited.

A catalog record of this book is available from the Library of Congress

ISBN 978-0-7566-9190-5

DK books are available at special discounts when purchased in bulk for sales promotions, premiums, fund-raising, or educational use. For details, contact: DK Publishing Special Markets, 375 Hudson Street, New York, New York 10014 or SpecialSales@dk.com.

Color reproduction by Colourscan
Printed and bound in Singapore by Tien Wah Press

Discover more at
www.dk.com

Contents

1 year to 18 months

19 months to 2 years

About the author

Dr. Claire Halsey is a consultant clinical psychologist of over 25 years' standing, specializing in work with children and families. A mother of three, she is a journalist and author in the field of child psychology, parenting and child development, recently co-authoring Dorling Kindersley's **Ask a Parenting Expert** (2009). She presented ITV's "**Driving Mum and Dad Mad**" and appears on parentchannel.tv, a parenting website supported by the Department for Education.

Introduction

Watching and supporting your baby's development is one of the greatest joys of parenthood. Each milestone is precious, from the moment your newborn looks into your eyes, to her first words, tentative steps, and through to achievements such as building a tower of blocks or creating a finger painting. You won't want to miss a thing.

Your baby is growing and developing at her fastest rate ever in these early months and you will notice changes in her on an almost weekly basis. It can be hard to keep up with all the new skills she's mastering, to know what will come next, and how best to support her progress. The information in these pages is designed to guide you through the steps of her development, keeping you informed about how her body and mind are working at each age and stage so you can be reassured that all is progressing as it should be.

In this book, I have drawn on my 25 years of work with children and families, studies of other experts in the field, and my own experience raising three boys to bring you the most detailed and up-to-date information about your baby's development. Alongside this account of what to expect are related play and activity suggestions to keep you and your baby stimulated, and learning together over her first two years.

You can use this book to check and track your baby's progress in the five key areas of social development, movement, hand control, communication, and brain power. These categories have been used to help organize this developmental information, however, most of your baby's activities give her practice in several areas at once. At a parent and toddler group, for example, your child will be developing socially as she plays next to others, she'll be communicating as she points at or tells you which toy she wants and will use her body, hands and brain power to play with the toys.

Of course, there is great variation in baby and toddler development with some infants reaching their milestones early while others take more time. However, if you begin to worry about your child's development, consult a health professional. In most cases you will be reassured that your baby or toddler is doing fine, but for some children early difficulties can be picked up and help and support offered.

Dr. Claire Halsey
AFBPsS, ClinPsyD, MSc, BA

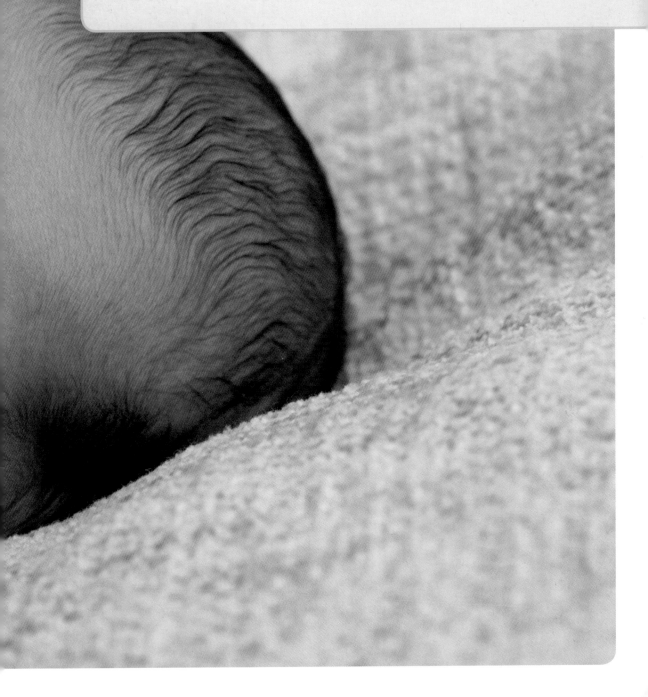

The first 2 months

YOUR NEW BABY

In the first few weeks of your baby's life, it may feel as though he does little other than eat and sleep. However, from the very beginning, your baby is growing rapidly and developing skills that will help him adjust to his new environment.

YOUR SOCIAL BABY

In the early weeks, your baby is completely focused on his relationship with you and any close family. He will respond by looking and turning toward those he sees often and is more likely to nestle into and be soothed by people who look, sound and smell familiar. From the beginning, his efforts are focused on making a connection with you: he'll make eye contact from the moment he is born, use different cries and body movements to bring you to his side, and show you that he loves to be close to you by quieting down when you hold him. At around six weeks of age, he'll reward you with his first smile, and will respond to your delight in it with many more.

In his first months, your baby experiences emotions as physical sensations that ripple through him. When this happens, he'll need you to hold and soothe him and reassure him with touch that he's safe, and that strong feelings don't have to be scary. He'll thrive when you tune in to his needs in this way.

GETTING MOVING

At birth, your baby has little control over his body—he can't control his head and most of his movements are reflexive, preprogrammed reactions to his world, such as the rooting reflex, whereby he turns his head whenever his cheek is stroked, ready to feed. These reflexes fade during his first three months. Although unable to control his movements

much at first, he'll soon start to put a great deal of practice and determination into developing his ability to move. His earliest goal will be taking control of his muscles and you will see him rapidly gain head and neck control in his first weeks.

HAND CONTROL

Your baby is ready to reach out from the moment he arrives. However, before his fine motor skills—his command of the movements made by the small muscles of his hands and fingers—can really take off, he has to wait for his preprogrammed grasp reflex to fade. This reflex means that he'll automatically wrap his fingers around yours when you press it into his hand, and so can't exercise conscious control over how he touches objects. He will, however, start to practice finer movements by reaching out with his arms, hands and fingers, and by as early as two months, he may be stretching out to touch a toy.

COMMUNICATION SKILLS

Your baby is a communication dynamo, motivated to understand you and be understood in return. In the early days, he communicates his needs mainly through crying. However, communication is much more than just the sounds your baby makes, and from early on he'll employ more subtle means of communicating through his body and gaze. From his very first moments, he'll be sending you messages about how he feels and what he wants by looking into your eyes and moving his body. You will complete the communication by sending a message back through your attention, gaze, gentle touch, and tone of voice. This two-way exchange forms the basis for turn taking, without which no communication or "conversation" can take place.

From early on, your baby will watch how your mouth moves and listen to the sounds you make. Watching your movements and enjoying the soothing tones of your voice is his first attempt to understand you, and in time to copy and replicate your actions.

Automatic The grasp reflex means your baby automatically grips anything in his palm. Enjoy the sensation as he grips your finger.

Smile At around six weeks, your baby shows his most engaging social skill—being able to smile genuinely at you.

BRAIN POWER

All the effort your baby makes to look, listen, and learn comes down to forging connections between his brain cells, or neurons. At birth, his brain is made up of over 100 billion of these cells, but it is the pathways between them that he needs to develop. These pathways, or connections, are there to pass information, and it is through them that learning occurs. As a newborn, some pathways are already formed, or hardwired, so your baby can immediately perform essential tasks such as turning his head, swallowing and sucking—his newborn reflexes. Many more must be created and strengthened by information from his senses. Everything he hears, sees, tastes, feels, or smells builds connections between brain cells. The more something happens, for example seeing your face or hearing you say his name, the stronger that neural pathway will be and the quicker he'll recognize things.

Over the next two years, your baby will discover some big ideas that allow him to think about and relate to his environment in different ways. The first of these is the notion of copying, the basics of this ability—to see something and imitate it himself—are present at birth and he'll use it nonstop in the coming months to practice new skills.

Up close and personal From birth, your newborn wants to look into your eyes and hold your gaze when you look lovingly back. It is through this powerful eye contact that you begin to communicate and forge a lasting connection.

Watching From the beginning, your baby observes constantly and absorbs information about her environment.

Key relations In these early months, your baby is busy forging relationships with the most important people in her world. Encouraging older siblings to spend time with her will help them to develop a close bond.

Your social baby

Strengthening your bond

Your newborn baby is ready for the most important relationships of her life—those she will share with you and your partner. Allowing yourself time to look at, touch, and get to know this tiny new person you've created, will give your relationship the best beginning possible.

How you're helping your baby

When you hold your baby close, look into her eyes and have skin-to-skin contact in the hours and days after the birth, you are helping her to:

★ Build the relationship between you. This bond sets the pattern for all her other relationships.

★ Feel secure. Her initial sense of safety comes from being held confidently by you.

★ Avoid distress. She's easily over-stimulated and your touch helps her calm herself.

★ Keep you close. She needs to know you are nearby to meet her needs.

★ Cry less. When your baby has skin-to-skin contact, she should cry less and bond more quickly with you.

Skin to skin Your newborn has been held safely inside you for nine months and can find the open space and freedom to move a shock at birth. Help her feel secure by holding her close, skin to skin if you can.

TOP TIP
The outside world is likely to be bewildering for your baby: make her first hours as comforting as possible through skin-to-skin contact, gentle touch and soft murmurings.

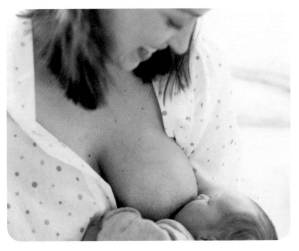

Feeding time Whether you offer the breast or bottle, your baby's feedings are an ideal time to focus on her. Make eye contact, respond by stroking her cheek if she stops sucking and enjoy being with her.

Dads too Skin-to-skin contact is an ideal way for dads to spend quiet time with their new baby and forge a strong connection, too. This is a father's equivalent to the closeness of breast-feeding.

Kangaroo care

Holding your baby skin-to-skin in the hours and days after the birth is also known as "kangaroo care," because it's similar to the way in which a baby kangaroo is carried by its mother.

Benefits of close contact Placing your baby on your chest or abdomen, with bare skin touching, can promote bonding and has proven benefits for premature babies' development. It's ideal just after the birth, but there's no time limit, so you and your partner can continue doing this in the weeks to come. It works best if you're relaxed and hold your newborn confidently, but lightly, as she lies on you. Cover her back with a blanket to keep her warm.

Kangaroo care is often recommended for premature babies. Studies have shown that premature babies who are held skin-to-skin put on weight more quickly and are better able to regulate their body temperature.

Warm and secure Lying on your body, skin next to skin, is an incredibly reassuring sensation for your new baby. After nine months cocooned inside the uterus, nestling close to your body helps her feel secure and safe.

Your social baby

Safe and secure

There is nothing as comforting to your baby as being snuggled, either with you, or in a blanket. Whether he likes being wrapped up, held in your arms, or tucked up in a crib, he'll be calmed by the feeling of safety.

How you're helping your baby

Swaddling, covering, and holding your baby close so he feels physically enclosed helps him:

★ **Feel safe and secure.** When you hold him, he's comforted by your familiar smell and is reassured by the sound of your voice. He's learning that you will always be there to comfort him.

★ **Fall asleep.** Having his body gently wrapped gives him a sense of safety and stops his automatic startle reflex movement (see p.27) from disturbing him during sleep.

★ **Get his fist to his mouth.** Swaddle him with a light blanket with his hands positioned near his mouth, so he can suck on them for comfort if he wants.

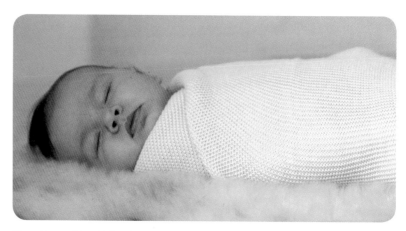

Wrap him up Some babies love to be swaddled because this recreates the feeling of being held firmly that they experienced before birth. Don't cover his head and check him regularly to ensure he doesn't get overheated.

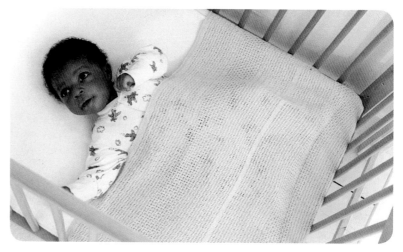

Helping sleep When your baby is tucked in well or enclosed he finds it easier to fall asleep. Swaddle him or tuck him in under a light blanket to give him a sense of being held.

KEY FACT
Making sure that you place your baby "back to sleep and feet to foot" (lie your baby to sleep on his back, with his feet positioned at the foot of his crib) is the best way to ensure safe sleeping.

Your social baby

Making eye contact

You are the center of your baby's world. He wants to focus on you in these first days and uses eye contact to connect with you. You won't be able to resist returning his gaze, strengthening your bond with each moment.

Fascinated by faces Your newborn prefers to look at faces more than any other picture or pattern, so give him lots of time just to stare at yours. Approach him slowly and murmur to let him know you are there as you bring your face close.

How you're helping your baby

When you hold your baby close, both facing you and supporting him to look around, you are helping him:

★ Bond with you. The looks you each give and receive help you get to know each other.

★ Learn about facial expressions and movements. His development of the art of copying, one of his learning tools, starts here.

★ Communicate how he feels. When you scan your baby's face, you are learning to read his expression and respond to his emotions.

★ Get to know his world. Everything he sees gives him information about patterns, colors, and movement.

I see you Your baby focuses best on objects about 8–10 in (20–25 cm) away. Position yourself with this in mind to give him a good view of your face, and then gaze back as he stares at you.

Copycat Within hours of the birth, your baby will be able to copy the movements of your face. While he's in a baby carrier or in your arms, let him see your face, then wait and watch while he tries to mimic you.

Your social baby

Mirroring

Life is an emotional roller coaster for your new baby. Love, happiness, fear, and frustration swoop through her as physical sensations. You're her mirror —showing her you can deal with her emotion helps her not to be afraid.

How these activities help your baby

When you accept your baby's feelings and mirror them back to her, you are helping her:

★ **Feel reassured** when strong feelings sweep through her body. She's learning not to be afraid of her emotions.

★ **Label her feelings.** When you put a name to each emotion you are beginning to teach her how to put feelings into words—she'll need this skill in the years to come.

★ **Show you how she feels.** You are learning to "read" her expressions, moods and body language; the more emotion she shows you, the more tuned in to her you will be.

Copying Mirror your baby's expression to teach about strong feelings. Reflect her emotion in a milder version, slightly tilting your head to signal understanding. Hold her while an emotion grips her to reassure her.

Naming emotions It's never too soon to name your baby's emotions for her. When she's expressing an emotion, talk about what is going on with comments such as "You look angry" or "Is that a sad face?".

Smile At around six weeks of age, when your baby surprises you with her first genuine smile, respond by grinning back and making a fuss. She'll know she's made a big impression and smile all the more.

Wow She's trying to read your face to learn what your expression means. When you exaggerate, perhaps with a big smile, wide eyes or lifting your eyebrows, she can see more clearly that you're happy or surprised.

TOP TIP
Keeping your baby close to you during the first weeks of life will enhance her bond with you, because you will be there to share in and name her new emotions.

Your social baby

First introductions

Meeting other parents and babies in the early months is good for your well-being and your baby's. For you, it's a chance to socialize and share parenting advice; for her, it's a new experience of being with other babies.

Be prepared Pack to entertain, distract, and comfort your baby. In addition to practical necessities, bring her favorite rattle and soft toys for her to suck and a blanket to tuck her up in if she gets fussy.

Who are you? Position your baby so she can see other children—she'll get to know them first through looking. Put her on a mat, in a bouncer, or hold her supported, facing outward if possible, so she can watch.

How these activities help your baby

When you introduce your baby to other children, you are helping her:

★ **Get used to other babies.** She's not ready to make friends, but the sound, sight and smell of other children will catch her interest.

★ **Meet future friends.** The children of your friends will be her future playmates.

★ **Experience something new.** A change of scenery opens her up to new sights, sounds and movements.

Family gatherings Getting together with close relatives provides the perfect opportunity for your baby to get to know both young and older members of the family—people who will be there for her as she grows up.

Slowly does it When you first socialize with your baby, stick to small groups and keep visits short. Judge how long to stay by your baby's reaction; this way she'll enjoy the experience without being overwhelmed.

Your social baby

Sibling relationships

Best of friends, protector, and playmate—brothers and sisters play plenty of roles with the youngest member of the family. Their initial adjustment to the new arrival can be tricky, though, and older children will need your help to get this relationship off to a good start.

How these activities help your children

When your older child is involved in caring for and playing with the new arrival, it helps them both:

★ **Feel close.** By spending plenty of time together, your children will get to know each other and form a bond.

★ **Begin to understand each other.** Two-way communication between your older child and your baby requires plenty of practice from them both.

★ **Realize they're both important.** Your older child needs to know he has a part to play in taking care of the new baby, so that he doesn't feel left out.

★ **Entertain each other.** They're going to be playmates.

★ **Reduce rivalry.** When your children have a strong bond, they're less likely to feel jealous or resentful of each other.

Little helper Involve your older child by giving him small chores. He can be your special helper, bringing a sponge or a toy, or helping you rock the baby in his bouncer.

Playtime Having fun together cements the relationship between your children, so encourage your older child to hold out toys for your baby to touch, swipe at, or watch.

Quiet time When your children have peaceful moments together, perhaps looking at a soft book or a toy, or simply exchanging looks and smiles, they're gradually gaining confidence in each other.

Gentle touch Teach your older child to gently touch and stroke your new baby by guiding her hand and letting her copy you. The more she gives and receives affection, the closer she'll feel to her sister or brother.

Special time Set aside a few minutes each day to focus all your attention on your older child. Snuggle up and read, enjoy a puzzle or get creative with a construction game. She'll share you more readily if she has you to herself sometimes.

Dealing with jealousy

Your older child has been the center of your attention and now he has to share this place with someone new. A degree of jealousy is only natural—but it's important not to let it get out of hand.

Give reassurance No matter how fairly you divide your time and involve the older child with your new one, at some point he will wish he could send the new baby back! He wants things to return to the way they were, so he may become more babylike himself to see if this does the trick. While this behavior may be irritating, don't scold him. He'll respond better with reassuring embraces and hugs.

Supervise carefully It's possible he'll get angry and rough with the new baby and might even hurt him without meaning to. He doesn't know his own strength or how vulnerable a young baby is. Handle this by closely supervising them together. For safety's sake, never leave an older child alone with a new baby, not even for a moment.

Have one-on-one time Understand your older child's temper and deal with it calmly, even when you feel upset—he won't resent the baby forever. Help your children get to know each other and remind your older child how special he is by giving him extra one-on-one attention. Eventually this phase will pass!

Your social baby

Loving massage

Getting to know your baby through touch boosts your bond. A daily dose of baby massage gives you the pleasure of focusing completely on her, helping you make a connection, as well as calming her with your touch.

Baby massage dos and don'ts

Follow these guidelines to ensure an enjoyable and relaxed massage.

Do begin to massage your baby in her first months. Some experts recommend waiting until she's six weeks old, while others suggest earlier. If you do massage before six weeks, avoid the umbilical stump area, since it may be tender.
Don't massage within 30 minutes of being fed, since stroking a full tummy can be uncomfortable for your baby.
Do massage your baby for at least 10 minutes for a relaxing experience.
Don't massage if your baby seems sick or has recently had immunizations. Consult a health professional if you have doubts.
Do choose a massage oil carefully. Pick edible, or plant-based, oils rather than those that are paraffin based. Avoid products that have scents or essential oils added, or ones that are likely to cause an allergic reaction, such as sesame or peanut oil.
Don't massage if your baby is turning away, squirming, or crying.
Do have your baby naked, or just in a diaper, for the massage, which means she'll need a warm room and a soft mat or towel to lie on. Dim the light in the room to enhance the sense of calm.

1 **Gently stroke your baby's face and head.** Run your fingertips over her forehead, cheeks, and lips and then stroke your fingertips from the sides of her nose out across her cheeks.

2 **Cup your hands over your baby's shoulders** and gently stroke her upper back and over her shoulders. Use circling movements and a gentle sweeping action.

3 **Very gently,** rub your baby's chest and abdomen with your palm. Move in a clockwise, then counterclockwise direction. If she shows any signs of discomfort, stop massaging this area.

4 **Hold your baby's hand** and gently straighten her arm. Use your other hand to stroke up and down her arm, using a soft "milking" action as you go. Repeat this on the other arm.

5 **Take your baby's hand** and give her palm a soothing stroke. Use a circling motion to work around each palm in turn, moving from the edges into the center.

6 **Take each finger in turn** and, with your thumb and forefinger, gently unfold the finger and then stroke it from the bottom to the fingertip. Finish with the thumb, then repeat on the other hand.

7 **Support your baby's ankle** in one hand, lift her leg slightly, and use your other hand to massage the leg from top to bottom. Lie it down gently and then take the other leg and repeat.

How you're helping your baby

When you massage your baby regularly, you help her:

★ Feel close to you. As you tune in to her through touch, your bond grows.

★ Be calm. You are soothing her with gentle rhythmic movements.

★ Cry less and sleep better. Your confidence in understanding her needs will help her become more settled.

★ Gain relief from gas and colic. Baby massage can help with these problems.

8 **Finish off with your baby's feet.** Hold her foot in your hand and massage the entire foot, working in circles over the sole and then gently pulling each toe. Repeat on the other foot.

Getting moving

New sensations

Your baby has so much to discover about his body. He's entranced by your touch, and loves the feel of different sensations. He's trying hard to figure out where his body ends and the rest of the world begins.

How these activities help your baby

When you touch, stroke, pat, and kiss your baby, you are helping him:

★ **Get feedback about how his body works.** He learns about how his body moves from sensory feedback: signals from his nerve endings, which travel to his brain, are created whenever you touch your baby.

★ **Enjoy his body.** Each gentle stroke or pat that you give your baby tells him that it's good to be touched.

★ **Give and take.** When you touch your baby, then wait a moment for him to respond, you are giving him time to register what he feels.

Softly, softly Stroke your baby's hair, cup her head with your hand or gently touch her face, and she'll gain a feeling of closeness. Support her head well while you stroke her, and she'll relax into your touch.

KEY FACT

Babies develop physically from the head down so you can expect your baby to have control over his head and neck before he can control the movement of his arms and legs.

Kiss, kiss Planting little kisses on your baby's hands and feet, holding his hand in yours, or letting him grasp your finger with his whole hand, all make him aware of these important parts of his body.

Do it again Your baby will love the rhythmic pat of your hand on his body. Be very delicate when you pat him—he'll want more of your feathery touch, and wiggle in delight to get you to continue.

Getting moving

Touch and tickle

Your baby is all action as he discovers his body can move. The motion of his arms, his wiggling body, and your playful games of touch and tickle, build his awareness of his trunk, arms and legs.

Tickle time Short bursts of gentle tickles are enjoyable for your baby and provide intense stimulation for his hands, feet, and body prompting him to move. He'll show you through his body language if he enjoys them or wants you to finish.

Words and action Your baby loves rhyme and touch combinations. The physical sensations on his skin, repeated over and over, give him great feedback about the position of his arms, legs, fingers, and toes.

Raspberries Gently blow a raspberry against the soft skin of your baby's tummy, then notice how he reacts, perhaps by waving his arms and legs, as this sensation tells him about his body. Repeat this as much as you want—as long as he seems to like it.

How these activities help your baby

When you build your baby's awareness of movement through playful games, you are helping him:

★ **Get to know his body** and how it moves. Feedback from his joints as he moves is important information for his developing brain.

★ **Practice moving.** The more your baby enjoys your games, the more he'll move and use his body.

★ **Become aware of his hands and feet.** When you play with his fingers and toes, he's beginning to learn that these are distinct parts of his body.

Getting moving

Encouraging motion

Your new baby is on a learning curve like no other as she tries to figure out how to turn, reach, and kick. At first she's at the mercy of reflex movements. A stimulating environment helps her learn to move her arms, legs, and body.

How these activities help your baby

When you give your baby plenty of opportunities to move her body, you are helping her:

★ **Enjoy big movements.** It's sheer pleasure to your baby to get her whole body moving.

★ **Use her muscles.** Your baby is ready to gain more conscious control over her arms and legs as the automatic reflex movements that she was born with begin to fade away.

★ **See her body as well as feel its movements.** Glimpses of her own moving arms and legs tell your baby about her body in motion, and helps the development of her hand–eye coordination in the coming months.

★ **Play games.** She will enjoy it when you join in and show your pleasure as she moves her body.

On the mat Giving your baby lots of floor time gives her plenty of opportunity to practice moving her limbs. She'll enjoy kicking her legs and waving her arms around.

Kick out Your baby will be attracted by toys and rattles attached to her mobile or baby gym and will try again and again to kick and wave her arms toward them.

KEY FACT
Your newborn's limbs will be curled to begin with, but you will gradually see them straighten as she flails her arms and kicks her legs, building muscle strength.

Both together When you keep your baby company at floor level or on a bed, and copy her movements, you'll realize what a workout she's getting. She'll move more because you're nearby, and when you describe what she's doing, she'll know you're focused on her.

Toe tickling Lightly brush your baby's toes with a soft, furry toy, or gently wave a noisy toy near her feet, and wait to see if she reacts. Your smiles and words of delight when she kicks out will spur her on to play this game again.

Avoiding too much stimulation

Even though your baby is eager for new experiences, it is possible to overstimulate her. Keep an eye on her reactions, and watch for signs that she's ready for rest.

How much is too much? She can become overwhelmed by too much playtime, or by too many toys or people. It's up to you to watch and judge when your baby is enjoying herself and when she's had enough.

When to play How well a baby responds to stimulation may depend on her temperament. Sensitive babies are easily overstimulated when there is a lot of activity or noise; more easy-going babies may be less fazed. It's up to you to decide when your baby has had enough.

When to stop Signs that it's time to back off include yawning, frowning, turning away, and starting to show distress. At these times, stop actively playing or offering her toys, and let her rest or take in her surroundings simply by looking quietly.

Take it slowly How you introduce toys and activities to your baby can enhance her enjoyment of them. She'll prefer it when you bring toys toward her slowly. You can imagine how a baby gym must seem huge to your baby, and she can easily be startled if it's put over her abruptly, or you put her on an activity mat too quickly. Approach her without rushing and she'll be receptive and more ready to play.

Hand control

Grasping and touching

Your baby is attracted by movement, light, and sound and turns toward and reaches for whatever is within range. He's desperate to get control of his arms, hands, and fingers so he can grab what he wants.

How these activities help your baby

Your baby still has little control over his movements, but he'll try to stretch out or wave his arms and grasp when you give him something to reach for. These opportunities help him:

★ Coordinate his movements. Each swipe and grab he makes gives his brain vital information about how his muscles and body move.

★ Keep trying. Successfully aiming at, reaching for, and grasping comes from repeating the same moves over and over again.

★ Get his eyes and hands working together. It is essential he practices looking and reaching together—his aim depends upon coordinating these.

★ Develop control of the small muscles of his hands and fingers. He is just starting to work on making these fine motor movements.

KEY FACT
Fine motor control follows less precise movements: your baby controls the movement of his arms and legs before he can control movement of his hands, fingers, and toes.

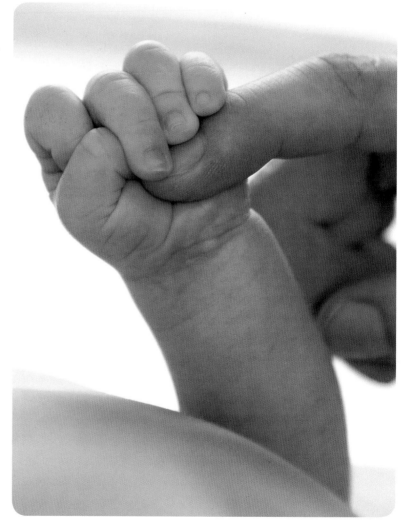

Hold on Your baby will automatically grip anything placed in his palm because his newborn grasp reflex is still in place. Give him the opportunity to grasp your finger or a rattle and he'll quickly figure out that waving a rattle makes a noise.

Squeaks and rattles Use every sort of small noisy toy, from a wrist rattle to squeaky squeeze toys to get his attention. He'll turn to the sound and his movements will help him locate the object responsible for the noise.

Newborn reflexes

Your baby has several preprogrammed reflexes that are necessary for his survival, such as sucking and swallowing. This means that he moves automatically in response to noise, touch, or movement, rather than through his own control.

Rooting, sucking, and swallowing These reflexes cause your baby to turn toward your touch if you stroke his cheek, and suck, then swallow, when anything is put in his mouth. They mean that he can take the breast or a bottle just as soon as he is born.

Step and startle These are reflexive body moves. Your baby will make stepping movements when his feet touch a hard surface, which may be practice for walking later; and his arms will fall outward if he feels unsupported, which helps to protect him from falls.

Grasp This reflex causes your baby to automatically grip anything put into his palm. It usually recedes at around 3 months, so he can then choose what he grips.

New sensations Feeling different textures will put your baby in sensory heaven and encourages him to explore, and eventually hold, objects. Give him a variety of fabrics and toys so he experiences things that are firm, soft, plush, crinkly, and spongy.

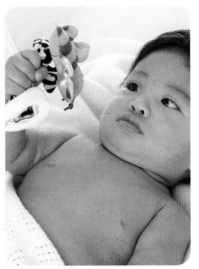

My hands He'll feel, mouth, and wave whatever goes into his hand. All this eye-catching movement kick-starts his fascination with his hands and fingers. They will continue to interest him over the coming months as he learns to manipulate objects.

27

Communication skills

Baby talk

You and your baby are a communicating powerhouse and in the coming months will be using every means possible to understand each other. Talking, singing, touching, and looking all teach your child something and start her on the path to expressing herself.

How these activities help your baby

When you sing, talk, touch, look, at and read to your baby, you are helping her:

★ **Understand the patterns and tones of speech** that form the basis for language.

★ **Learn to listen and respond.** This starts the two-way dance of communication.

★ **Use touch to gain your attention.** This helps to bring you closer, and keep you in "baby talk" range.

★ **Practice copying.** She will see how you move your face and mouth, which is essential for nonverbal communication.

★ **Gain a larger vocabulary.** The more you talk to her now, the greater her vocabulary will be in the future.

★ **Enjoy communicating.** She will want to express herself, and relax in the confidence that you will respond to her needs.

Funny faces From the beginning, your baby observes your face and mouth as you talk. Make exaggerated facial movements while talking to her—learning to move her mouth like you is the precursor to her baby babble.

Singing Your baby will love it when you sing to her. Choosing songs that rhyme gets your baby used to the patterns and sounds of words. This will help her later as she learns to speak and then to read.

Talking to your baby Coo, murmur, and talk to her. Give a running commentary of what you are doing and describe what you can see. Begin talking as soon as your baby is born; it will come naturally to you.

Backward is best Using a backward-facing baby carrier or stroller makes it much easier to speak to your baby and tune in to her emotions and reactions because you can see her face and she can see yours.

Touching you When she reaches out to touch you, move closer to let her explore, smile, and make eye contact to reinforce her connection with you.

Communication skills

Reading his signals

Your baby gives you constant clues about how he feels, and is waiting for you to figure them out. When he cries, coos, scowls, waves his arms, or kicks his legs, watch and listen and you'll soon learn what he means.

How you're helping your baby

When you read your baby's signals, you are helping him:

★ **Get what he needs to survive.** Each communication from him tells you what he needs so you can do something about it.

★ **Realize communication works.** As he signals and you respond, he gets the important message that communicating is worth the effort.

★ **Feel secure.** When you go to him as soon as he cries, he knows that he can rely on you.

★ **Get into a routine.** As he develops, notice which times of day he wants his feedings, sleep, and play, and start to plan a routine around them.

Needing attention Listen carefully and you will notice that your baby has several distinct cries that vary in tone and intensity and have different meanings. In his first weeks, you will begin to recognize which cry means "I'm hungry" or "I'm tired."

KEY FACT
A recent study found that babies who are held a lot and fed on demand will cry less each day, on average, than those who receive less physical contact and have a stricter schedule.

Peace and quiet There are times to play and times to be quiet. Keep playing if your baby appears alert, looks at you, coos, and raises his arms. Stop if he keeps turning his head away, cries, yawns, or frowns.

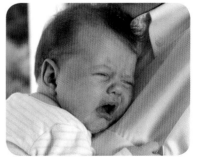

Hold me close Quite often your baby will be overwhelmed by strong emotions. All you can do is hold him close, murmur reassurance, and rock or stroke him, while he lets the intense feeling grip him.

Time for sleep Watch out for signs that your baby is tired. Perhaps he pulls at his ear or rubs his eyes. As soon as you notice these gestures, settle him down. If you wait too long, he'll be overly tired, which makes it harder to fall asleep.

Calm and content As you gain confidence in "reading" his sounds, cries and body language, you will get steadily better at recognizing his needs and reacting quickly to meet them. A contented baby—at least some of the time—will be the result.

Your baby's first smile

It might seem a long time to wait but you are likely to see your baby's first real social smile at about four to six weeks.

No turning back Up until now, it's been his cries that have drawn you to him but once he starts smiling he has a much more pleasing way of getting your attention. It is no coincidence that the amount of time he spends crying—about two hours each day when he's three to six weeks old—gradually reduces as his ability to engage you with a smile begins.

The real thing Your baby's smile is genuine—he is truly happy to see you and he'll be overjoyed if you make a big fuss in return. "Ooh" and "aah" at his achievement and smile right back at him. When you return your baby's smile, you are showing him that communication is a two-way thing—he tells you he is happy by smiling and you reflect that back to him by smiling too.

Brain power

Learning through looking

Your new baby can focus just a short distance, so she's fascinated by faces. She loves bold patterns and prefers black and white pictures and designs. As her eye muscles strengthen, her view of the world improves.

How these activities help your baby

When she has a plentiful supply of things to look at, you are helping her:

★ **Focus.** Bright, clear patterns help your baby practice focusing her eyes, and develop the visual area of her brain.

★ **Figure out her senses.** At first, the pathways in her brain for different senses are hard for her to separate. She may experience a loud noise as a disturbance of her vision, as well as hearing it.

★ **Follow a moving object with her eyes.** Keeping her eyes on a toy as it moves slowly past her is her newest skill.

★ **Learn about color.** Although she likes black and white patterns, your baby needs to see more than black and white to learn about her world. Introduce her to color with colorful toys and decor.

Contrast It's easier for her to see patterns with strong contrasts between shades. Catch her eye with books, mobiles, or toys with clear black and white designs.

Is that me? Your baby watches her image, but she won't recognize it as herself until she's six months old or more. Hold her in front of a mirror or give her a mirrored toy.

KEY FACT

Connections in your baby's brain—synapses—are formed in direct response to the stimulation she receives from you: synapse creation is at its peak up to the age of three.

Bright and breezy She's naturally attracted to things that are moving, shiny, and bright. Colorful mobiles, toys that vibrate or anything interesting in her line of vision gives her practice in the essential skill of watching, or tracking, objects as they move.

Your face From the moment she's born, your baby would rather look at faces than anything else. Let her stare at your face as she feeds, and show her bold pictures of faces with different expressions and watch to see which ones she likes, or gazes at, the most.

How your baby's sight develops

At birth, your baby can focus best from a distance of 8–10 in (20–25 cm), but her vision is blurry. Over the weeks, her focus and abillity to see detail will improve. By eight months she'll see almost as well as you do.

Making connections A lot of your baby's visual ability comes through the development of her brain. As she repeatedly sees bold patterns, colors and movement, her neural or brain cells form pathways and she begins to recognize often repeated patterns. Her depth perception develops through these same pathways by around three to five months of age. Before this, experts believe that babies see in two dimensions, rather than three.

Eye coordination At birth your baby can't always get both eyes working together. You may notice that her eyes wander or turn in at times. By about three months old, she'll be able to track a moving object using both eyes with ease. If you do notice her eyes are consistently turned in or out, get advice from a health professional.

Seeing color Babies are able to make out color, at least red and green, by about two weeks of age. At first they struggle to distinguish between similar tones, such as red and orange, but between two and four months, color differences become more clear.

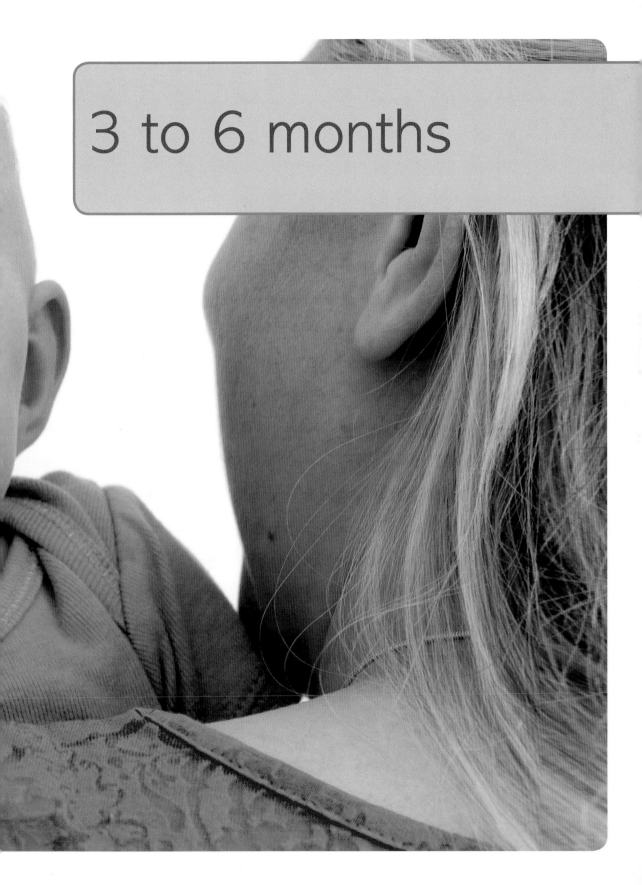

3 to 6 months

YOUR GROWING BABY

From three months, your baby's personality really starts to shine through as she uses both her voice and body language to express herself. Her mobility accelerates now, and once she learns to roll, she will take a far more active interest in her world.

YOUR SOCIAL BABY

From one person to many, your baby's social circle grows steadily month by month, as does her awareness and recognition of herself and those around her. However, you are at the heart of her world, and your relationship with her forms the basis for her sense of security, her confidence to branch out and play, and sets the pattern for how she relates to others. By three months, she'll smile at strangers as well as her close circle, and stare intently at other babies. Her social skills expand quickly as she learns to give and receive affection, babble, and anticipate events. As early as six months, she can recognize simple emotions, crying if someone cries and reacting to your tone of voice.

GETTING MOVING

Your baby wants to move and is motivated by the simple satisfaction of being able to control her body. Her physical development starts from her head and moves down and outward, with control of her hands and fingers, legs, and feet coming last.

During this period, her stronger head control enables her to push up with her arms during tummy time, and shortly after this, she'll gain sufficient strength and coordination to master the art of rolling.

HAND CONTROL

Your baby is driven to feel, grab, hold, and move the people and objects she can see and hear. You'll see her fierce concentration as she tries to gain control of the muscles of her arms, hands and fingers to reach what she wants. Finally, at around three months, with plenty of persistence and practice, she will consciously choose to grip an object, and will then be able to start really finessing her small hand movements.

However, controlling these movements is only half the task as she tries to grab a toy. Her growing ability to focus on and follow objects with her eyes is essential for her to aim her arms and hands accurately, known as hand–eye coordination. Her eyesight develops rapidly in line with her fine motor control, and by the time she's three months old, you'll notice her looking intently at her hands as she reaches for a toy. While she was ready to stretch out for toys as early as two months, it's not until around three months that she starts to grasp them.

COMMUNICATION SKILLS

As your baby learns to move her mouth to make a noise, she'll soon start to gurgle and babble. As she reaches three months, she'll make vowel sounds such as "o" and "e" and

Holding on As your baby's grasp improves, she'll love to handle and explore books and toys with different textures.

Letting her touch When she reaches out to touch you, move closer to let her explore. Smile at her to reinforce this connection.

Make things happen As your baby learns about cause and effect, give her toys that help her see that her actions lead to a reaction.

plenty of squeals and gurgles. Her babbling will really take off after this and you'll notice lots of repetition, such as "ba ba ba," and "ka ka ka." Alongside her babbles, she's busy listening and learning so she can receive communication as skillfully as she gives it.

In addition to vocalizing, your baby will find more ways to communicate how she feels. By three months, she'll tell you what she likes through smiles, turning her head toward you, and wiggling with pleasure. Her dislikes will show up as crying, flushing, and frantic waving of her arms and legs.

BRAIN POWER

Your baby's brain is developing at the fastest rate it ever will—she is primed and ready to learn. Everything that she sees, touches, tastes, smells, and hears, builds her knowledge of her world. You're her number one teacher, giving her the chance to explore and experience new things and being there along the way to explain it all.

By three to four months, she also starts to learn a key concept. She'll begin to notice that her actions can make something happen, for example, if she cries you'll come to her, or if she swipes a toy it moves. This is cause and effect and her grasp of this concept helps her understanding of the world.

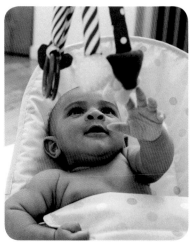

I want it Your baby is starting to reach out and aim for things. Encourage her by offering bright and noisy toys to swipe at.

Lifting her head As your baby's neck muscles continue to strengthen, she will lift her head for longer when on her tummy. Put toys that move or make a noise in front of or near her so she wants to look up and around.

Your social baby

Quiet moments

You and your baby are developing a great partnership. It takes time and patience to get to know each other, so create and treasure moments of quiet connection when you have little to do except be together.

How these activities help your baby

When you and your baby share quiet times, you are helping her:

★ **Get to know you.** Peaceful occasions allow the two of you to concentrate on each other, strengthening the bond that is growing between you.

★ **Build her social skills.** Without toys and noise to distract your baby constantly, she can practice simply watching and responding to you.

★ **Share an experience.** Social connections are created through spending time together. These shared experiences form an essential part of your relationship.

★ **Feel safe to look and listen.** When you are close by, you form the safe base from which she can observe the world.

Happy doing nothing Just being together can be enough sometimes. Your baby takes in your smile, your smell, and the feel of your touch when you set aside time to do nothing except enjoy each others' company.

KEY FACT
Spending quiet time in close contact with your baby helps her bond with you. It also allows her to have calm moments—vital for avoiding overstimulation.

Just looking When you quietly watch the world go by, you are relaxing in a shared moment. Hold your baby as she enjoys the view, and appreciate her small movements, and expression if something catches her eye.

Share the view Sit on a rug under the trees and look at the leaves moving above you, or cradle your baby as you watch and listen to a wind chime. Talk about it later, saying "We saw beautiful leaves today."

Your social baby

Meeting and greeting

Your social baby loves company and knows how to show it. She is ready to let her hands do the talking as she greets you by reaching for cuddling and watches when you beckon, wave, or give a thumbs–up. Your gestures get her involved with social situations, and she'll be eager to mimic you.

Point it out She's not quite ready to point, but it's time to show her the gesture. Use your index finger to prod or point clearly to a toy or picture. Increase the distance between finger and toy as she gets the idea.

Coming and going Waving goodbye as someone leaves is one of our most common gestures: your baby will love to watch and copy. Hold her as you wave; lift her hand to wave too and she'll soon try this on her own.

How these activities help your baby

As your baby watches how you meet and greet, you're helping her:

★ Join social customs. Gestures are often used to mark the beginning or end of social situations.

★ Understand social situations. Learning when and why gestures are used helps her to "read" and understand others.

★ Get into good habits. Waving and greeting people with affection are good manners and she'll copy them from you.

★ Practice. Precise gestures take muscle control and hand–eye coordination; she gains these through plenty of practice.

Hold me close Your baby may not be able to talk yet, but she'll reach out and touch your face in a greeting to show her pleasure when you draw her close to you.

I need you Show her gestures such as beckoning and reaching to be picked up and encourage her to copy. She is naturally motivated to communicate with you through these important signals.

Your social baby

Getting to know family

Your baby has been totally engrossed in his relationship with you until recently, but now he's ready to expand his social circle. It's time for you to introduce him to more people and help him to strengthen the bonds with his brothers, sisters, and other close family members.

How these activities help your baby

As you involve your wider family in your baby's life, you're helping him:

★ **Widen his safety net.** Your whole family, from siblings and grandparents to aunts, uncles, and cousins, provide a caring network for your baby.

★ **Be willing to leave you.** Familiarity with other people reduces your baby's distress when they handle, hold, or even babysit him.

★ **Establish bonds for a lifetime.** Your baby is starting long-lasting relationships with his own generation, whether it's his brother, sister, or cousin.

★ **Engage his social skills.** Your baby is ready to practice his smile and babbles on a new audience to see if they respond to him too.

Share a game As you introduce a new relative, hold your baby and give him time to gaze at the person. Get the relative to share a story or play a rhyme game such as "Itsy-bitsy Spider." When you join in too, your baby feels safe to socialize.

KEY FACT
By about four months your baby will recognize you and his siblings, who are likely to delight in his spontaneous smiles and frequent giggles.

Small gatherings It's easy to overwhelm your baby, so introduce him to small groups and keep visits short. He'll be interested in others when he's feeling alert, so time new introductions to match his mood.

Pick me up It's a sure sign of her growing ease when your baby reaches out to family members for holding and comfort. Step back and give relatives a chance to get close and spend time with your baby.

Best friends Guide your child to watch her baby sister's or brother's reaction as she makes a face or offers a toy. Point out how he is signaling by looking, smiling, and moving his body. As they respond to each other, their bond grows.

Getting moving

Tummy time

It's good to be well-rounded, and for your baby that means getting play time and exercise on her tummy as well as lying on her back. She'll use tummy time to push against the floor with her hands and toes, lift her head, and strengthen muscles that don't get a workout at other times.

How these activities help your baby

By giving your baby generous amounts of tummy time, you are helping her:

★ **Get ready to roll.** Your baby will start to practice movements, such as pushing up, that are vital to rolling and crawling.

★ **Lift her head.** Lying on her front is an ideal position for strengthening her neck muscles, an essential for head control.

★ **Tolerate something new.** Keep trying tummy time: start by leaving her on her front for a few moments, and gradually extend the time. This teaches her to deal with setbacks as she gets used to this new experience.

Head up Encourage your baby to lift her head briefly by calling her name and making noises with a toy to the front and slightly above her. When you direct her attention upward, her head will come up, too.

Make the effort Tummy time can be hard work. Place toys or mirrors so she can see them when she lifts up. Lie on your back and put her face down on your tummy while you hold her: she'll push up to look into your face.

Getting comfortable At first, tummy time may feel unfamiliar and frustrating and she won't like that she can't see you easily. Lie facing her and hold her interest by blowing raspberries, making faces, and offering toys.

TOP TIP

Use a firm, comfortable surface for tummy time. Avoid pillows or soft materials that could hamper breathing. Supervise her closely, too, since she shouldn't fall asleep on her front.

Getting moving

Diaper-free play

Your baby is wild about movement, but can feel restricted by clothes and his bulky diaper. Let his limbs loose every now and then, and he'll enjoy the new sensations on his skin and greater freedom of movement.

How these activities help your baby

Giving your baby some diaper- and clothes-free time helps him:

★ **Move freely.** He'll enjoy a full range of movement with no clothes to limit him.

★ **Get a grip.** He needs to be able to use his toes to push himself around.

★ **Gain coordination.** The more he sees his body move, as well as feels it, the better his hand–eye coordination.

★ **Enjoy himself.** It's exciting for your baby to move his body.

Work out Your baby will enjoy working his body when you offer a bit of resistance. Before putting on a new diaper, lightly push against the soles of his feet as he moves his legs or guide him in a "cycling" motion to refine his actions.

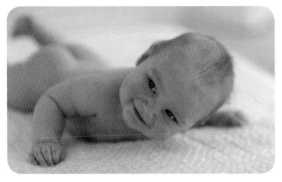

I'm free With no diaper, socks, or onesie, your baby can really feel his body working against the floor. Put him on his tummy and he will pull up his knees and dig in his toes to push against the carpet, both of which are great preparation for crawling.

My body It's a pure pleasure for your baby simply to move freely without restrictions and see his body in action. Draw his attention to his hands, arms, feet, and legs by naming them as he moves around to give him even more information about his body.

Getting moving

Physical play

Your baby is in his element when you swoop him into different positions. As his head control strengthens, he'll love to bounce, rock, and twist in your arms, improving his balance and body awareness in the process.

How these activities help your baby

By supporting your baby as his body moves in different directions, you are helping him:

★ **Develop better balance.** Movements set off the motion sensors in his ear canal, which stimulate the parts of his brain responsible for balance.

★ **Strengthen his head control.** Holding his head and body at different angles works his neck muscles hard.

★ **Acquire body awareness.** Your baby is finding out how his body moves through space and he's working toward a big milestone—rolling over.

Different angles Hold your baby firmly in your arms or supported on your knee, then gently lift him to give him the experience of moving up and down. He'll bend his knees in response and help you to bounce him.

Bouncing As her coordination and head control improve, she'll enjoy bouncing. Sit her on your knees and lift them to bounce her, or pop her in a doorway bouncer and watch her push herself off.

TOP TIP

Follow the safety instructions with a doorway bouncer. Use it only when your baby has gained good head control and stick to 10–15 minute sessions.

Almost dancing It's great exercise for your baby's muscles when his body is held and moved at different angles. As long as he is wrapped in your arms or held securely, he will feel safe even if he's slightly off balance.

Turn around Hold him close and slowly and smoothly turn around: the twirling sensation will be new to him and pleasant when it's unhurried. But don't go too fast or make jerky movements—they won't please.

How movement encourages coordination

Every move your baby makes floods his brain with information that helps to develop his coordination.

Stimulating nerves To improve and refine his movement, your baby's biggest need is feedback from his senses. Whenever he moves, the nerve endings in his joints, on the surface of his skin and where his body touches the floor, provide feedback that helps his brain develop a "map" of his body and its movements.

Stronger muscles Physical activity, from leg waving to pushing up during tummy time, strengthens his muscles so they can move smoothly together. Repeating any movement over and over again reinforces the messages to the brain about how each arm, leg, hand, or foot works together, which in turn helps to develop coordination.

Practice makes perfect As your baby tries new moves and persists in reaching for a toy, or digging in with his toes to push himself forward, he's creating patterns in his brain, which make his moves just a little easier each time.

Body and mind This isn't just about movement. When information about the position and action of his head, body and limbs is matched to what he can see, then he's on track to accurately aim for and reach a toy or launch himself toward you.

Fantastic feedback Support your baby's head and rock him side to side, up and down, or angled across your body to create different sensations. All of these actions help him gain awareness of his body and the space it occupies in the world.

Getting moving

Push-ups

Your baby is on a mission to get mobile, and each move she makes builds toward this goal. Pushing up and taking her weight, or working on balance all help her reach the milestones of rolling, crawling, and standing.

How these activities help your baby

Moving her body is fun, but it can be hard work for your baby. With your encouragement, you're helping her:

★ **Practice.** It is through repeating moves time and again that she finally masters them.

★ **Put her moves together.** A seemingly simple task, such as looking for, reaching for, and grasping a toy, means that your baby has to get many different body parts working at the same time.

★ **Reach her goal.** Your baby is striving to move her body, and will get immense satisfaction when she inches forward or gets the toy she's aiming for.

Up and looking Pushing up her head and chest is a vital building block for crawling. Encourage her by holding a toy in front and a bit above her, and reward her with smiles and claps. Try tummy time in your yard so there's more to see once she's up.

KEY FACT
Tummy time is vital: it encourages your baby to lift herself up and eventually crawl; it allows her to get used to a different position; and it helps her body develop evenly.

Taking some weight As you bear most of her weight, let your baby push up with her feet; very slightly sway her so that she can feel weight on one foot, then the other. Her muscles and balance will benefit.

I'm flying Gently challenge your baby's balance. "Fly" her on your legs or lie her on your tummy and rock slightly so she has to use her arms and legs to steady herself. Hold her securely so she knows she won't fall.

Getting moving

Gaining strength

Your baby demands a lot of her muscles as she plays, pushes up, and reaches. She'll get tired and frustrated at times, and be totally absorbed at other times as her body begins to work in the way she wants it to.

Working all angles Your baby needs to strengthen different muscle groups equally for them to operate together well. Time on her tummy, back or upright works her back and front. Encourage her to look and reach to left and right so each side develops evenly.

How these activities help your baby

When your baby gets the chance to practice big movements in plenty of different positions, you are helping her:

★ **Develop evenly.** Both the left and right sides and the back and front of her body need to strengthen evenly at the same pace to help her roll, crawl, and then, eventually, walk.

★ **Make smooth movements.** As her muscles strengthen, her movements are steadier and less jerky.

★ **Get ready to sit.** Your baby needs strong muscles in her trunk and legs to give her the stability to sit unsupported.

Reach out At about six months, her increased strength means her muscles hold her while she practices smaller movements. On her tummy, or supported in a playnest, put a toy just out of reach: she'll have the strength to stay steady while she grabs it.

Stand up! The large muscles of your baby's legs support her weight and will help her roll and crawl. Strengthen these muscles by holding her securely while she stands on your legs and bends her knees.

Getting moving

Water baby

Start your baby's adventure with water early. Give him playful times in the bath tub, paddling pool, at swimming class or just splashing around with water in a bowl. Your aim is for him to be relaxed and confident around water and to enjoy the feel of it on his face and body.

How these activities help your baby

As you play with water together or take your baby swimming, you're helping him:

★ **Improve his coordination.** He can try out movements that, on land, he wouldn't have the muscle strength or control to manage.

★ **Work his muscles.** Every kick, glide, and splash builds his muscle strength: water play will tire him out.

★ **Build his confidence.** Whether he's in his bath or the pool, he'll be more comfortable getting wet or splashed if he plays in water regularly.

Splish, splash Give your baby the satisfaction of making a splash. Pop toys in the water for him to kick, or pat down on the water to make a big splash. Focusing on the effects he can make with the water will help him to refine his movements.

KEY FACT

Your baby won't have the coordination to swim for a couple of years, but getting him confident and relaxed around water is important for both of you.

Swim class Sign up for a baby swimming class. You'll be taught how to help your baby move in the water and keep her safe. Find out about classes from other parents, mommy-and-me classes, or at a recreation center.

Summertime fun Once she can sit without support, a paddling pool is great fun in hot weather. Get in with her and watch as she enjoys the reflections on the water, and the breeze on her skin.

Freedom to move When your baby is weightless in the water, so many movements are easier. Glide him in the water, and guide him through movements that, on land, would be too difficult. He'll love being pulled toward you for a watery hug.

Taking your baby swimming

It is up to you when you want to take your baby swimming. Many baby swimming classes begin at 12 weeks old, although some health professionals recommend waiting until six months, when your baby has greater head control and muscle strength.

Immunizations Your baby doesn't need to have been immunized, since the chlorine in the water kills any bugs and viruses. But when very young he might feel overwhelmed in a large swimming pool.

Pool hygiene Your baby should always wear a swim diaper in a public pool.

Water temperature Your baby loses body heat quickly, so the water should be sufficiently warm—around 86–89.6° F (30–32° C) is recommended.

Safety Always supervise your baby closely and never leave him unattended in or near water—not even for the shortest amount of time. Babies can drown in less than a minute in just a few inches of water.

When not to swim Do not take your baby swimming when he's sick, or for 48 hours after he has had vomiting or diarrhea. Check with a health professional if you have any doubts.

Getting moving

Looking and stretching

Your baby is thirsty for different perspectives—to see things from above and underneath, and while she's on the move. Frequently changing her position keeps her stimulated and encourages movement.

How these activities help your baby

When she's free to move, reach, and stretch in different positions you are helping your baby:

★ **Strengthen different parts of her body.** Your baby has to work a slightly different set of muscles every time you change her position.

★ **Coordinate her body.** As your baby changes her position, she's building strength in her trunk and improving her coordination.

★ **Balance.** Each different angle gives your baby new information about her body's position and helps her work on balancing in each posture.

TOP TIP
Babies spend less time now on their tummies, missing out on an important position for developing arm and neck strength. Include this play position in your baby's daily routine.

Sit and play Prop your baby up so she has a stable position, then give her noisy, bright rattles to reach for, get her to lean forward to clap your hand, or put a cloth over her legs so she stretches to pull it off. Each time she leans out she's refining her balance.

Look and move Give your baby things to look at and play with during tummy time to keep her motivated to stay there. She'll stare happily at a book or baby mirror, turn her head when you squeak a toy near her, and push up to see you when you call.

Sharing a view Lie with your baby to see how she views the world. She'll love it if you copy her movements and will copy you in return. Lie in places you wouldn't usually—maybe under a table, reaching your toes up to touch it, or outside on a blanket.

Keep moving Your baby's movements are more limited when she's sitting in a car seat, stroller, or bouncer seat, so keep it balanced by giving her plenty of time in your arms, or unrestricted on the floor, so she can make big movements.

Yoga for babies

Baby yoga classes enable parents and babies to exercise together. They involve gentle stretching and movement, breathing exercises, and relaxation techniques to encourage coordination and flexibility.

Benefits of baby yoga The gentle physical activity aims to intensify the bond between the two of you, help your baby settle down and sleep better, and give you a feeling of relaxation. The focus is on the movements, as well as relaxation, as both you and your baby practice moves and postures together. It also helps you gain confidence handling your young baby and can increase your baby's awareness of her body and confidence as she grows.

When to start Baby yoga classes are appropriate when your baby is around 12 to 16 weeks, although opinion varies and some groups start as early as newborn.

What you'll need Check whether the class has mats since you'll need to take one for you and one for your baby, as well as your usual baby bag.

Safety guidelines You shouldn't take your baby to baby yoga if either she, or you, is sick. Also, if you or your baby have ongoing medical problems, you should consult a health professional to discuss whether baby yoga is recommended.

Getting moving

Rolling over

Your baby is about to reach a major movement milestone—rolling over. He'll be as surprised as you when his wiggles and reaching tip him over and he's rolled from his back to his front.

KEY FACT
Being able to roll depends on your baby's head control, neck, and arm strength. Some babies can roll at three months, while others aren't ready until six or seven months.

How these activities help your baby

By encouraging your baby in the steps that lead to rolling, you're helping him:

★ Build his strength. He needs strong stomach muscles to roll over.

★ Practice. Opportunities to rock his body, push with his feet and reach out help him learn to roll over.

★ Experience new movements. When you support him in a roll, he's getting to know the sensation of his body turning.

★ Develop his body evenly. Letting him play and reach to either side equally ensures even muscle development.

Surprise! Your baby may be a little shocked as well as happy about rolling over. Let her know through your enthusiastic praise that rolling is a good thing, then gently turn her over to try again.

1 **Once your baby's neck and arm** muscles are sufficiently strong, he will be able to lift his arm and bring it over his body, turning his whole body onto its side as he does.

2 **With his upper body turned,** your baby will start to coordinate the movement in his legs, lifting his leg up and to the side and then swinging it over completely to the floor.

3 **Now that he has successfully rolled over** from his back to his front, he can happily push himself up on his arms. It won't be long before he's crawling and fully mobile!

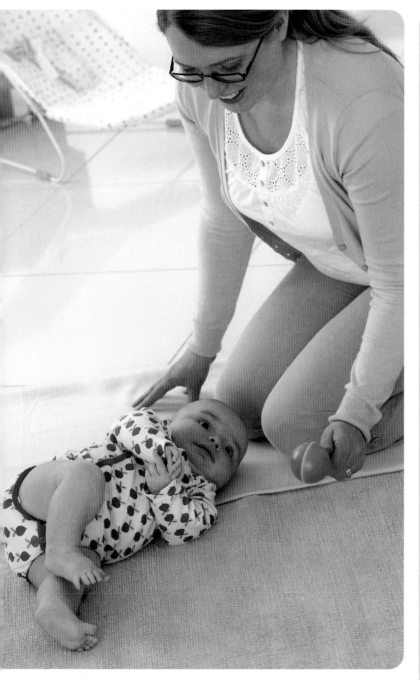

Move a toy Give your baby good reason to turn onto his side by moving a toy to the side near the top of his head, so he has to turn to keep it in sight. Rolling from a smooth to a textured surface helps him realize he has moved his body to a new place.

Keeping your explorer safe

Once your baby starts to roll, he's on the move! Creating a safe environment gives him the freedom to explore and exercise his curiosity without constant reprimands to stay away from this or that.

Babyproof your home Look at it from his point of view. Crawl around and you'll notice the sharp edges of tables at baby eye level, appealing electrical outlets, and knobs on the stove for little fingers to explore once he starts to pull up. All of these dangers can be tackled with close supervision and by using safety gadgets, such as stair gates and child locks.

Lock poisons away Many household products are poisonous, but to your baby the bright, shiny packaging and nice smell is appealing. Products such as cleaning fluids and sprays, alcohol, and medicines should be kept in a cupboard, drawer, or medicine chest with a child lock.

Make your yard baby friendly Safety check your yard, shed, and garage and lock away chemicals, sharp tools, and anything else that could hurt your baby. Check flowerbeds for poisonous plants and remove any that your baby could put in his mouth.

Avoid any risks Don't leave your baby for a moment in situations where his curiosity could put him in danger. Be especially vigilant when your baby is eating, or is in or near water.

Learn life-saving skills If you haven't already done so, take a first-aid training course to learn what action to take in an emergency.

Getting moving

Sitting and reaching

Your baby is trying hard to sit up, even though she wobbles and may topple over. Once she can sit without falling, she has a stable base from which she can reach out and use her hands to explore her surroundings.

How these activities help your baby

When you encourage your baby while she's sitting, you're helping her:

★ **Build trunk strength.** Your baby needs strong back and stomach muscles to hold herself in a sitting position.

★ **Experiment.** She's figuring out by trial and error how far forward she can lean without tipping over.

★ **Gain control.** Once your baby has a firm base, she can direct her arms and hands to go where she really wants.

Keep trying Being able to sit, and not fall over, takes practice. As your baby gains strength and balance, give her chances to sit without support to see if she can stay upright. Be ready to catch her if she topples.

KEY FACT
Greater neck and chest strength allow your baby to sit, although not get into a sitting position. She will learn to lean forward without falling, then gain the confidence to sit alone.

Soft landings There is no way around it, she will tip over many times while she's learning to sit. Avoid too many bumps and bruises by giving her a soft landing—that way she'll be ready to try again without too many tears.

Stretching for toys Being able to sit with support and even sit alone by six months requires strength and balance. Build these up by placing toys in different positions around him so he stretches and turns to get them.

Hand control

Learning to grab

Your baby wants to grab everything—and now he can. He's beginning to develop more conscious control over his movements and is ready to swipe at and grasp whatever catches his eye.

How these activities help your baby

When you offer your baby a variety of noisy, bright, soft, bumpy, and moving toys, you are helping him to:

★ **Keep trying.** At first your baby will miss the toy he's trying for most of the time, but with plenty of practice he will improve his aim.

★ **Develop his brain.** Each movement your baby makes strengthens the connections in his brain, which allow him to perfect fine movements.

★ **Look and grab.** Your baby's eyes and hands must work together for him to see what he wants, aim for, and reach it.

Aiming high You can see the determination in your baby as he swipes at toys on his baby gym or stroller, or those you dangle above him. Don't worry if he's not accurate: each time he swings out, he's making tiny improvements to his aim.

Look up Your baby needs to be able to focus on and follow moving objects with his eyes to be able to grab them. Hang a mobile over his crib, hold him up to look at wind chimes or roll a ball so he can track it and reach out.

Hear, see, swipe Noisy toys are good attention grabbers, getting your baby to look, reach, and turn. Scrunch a crinkly toy or paper above and next to him to attract him and encourage him to reach and grab.

In his grasp Being able to open his hand and curl his fingers around a toy are tricky movements, and your baby will be delighted when he does this. Hold a toy near his hand and wait for him to open his palm to grasp it.

Easy-grip toys Give your baby a helping hand by offering toys that are easy to grip. Small, soft toys, rattles, and toys with knobs and bumps give him plenty to get hold of, so he's more likely to be successful in picking them up.

How your baby's hold develops

By the time he's three months old, your baby is using his hands for all sorts of activities.

Loss of newborn reflexes Your baby's grasp reflex has faded, and he'll be able to open and close his hands at will and grip or press them together. He's busy learning all about them and what they can do.

Aiming at his target His first attempts at picking up an object will be to swipe at it, possibly touching it with his fingers, but not getting his aim quite right. He'll keep on trying, though, and each swing helps him match what he sees with where his hand is going.

Improved control By four or five months, he will have better control of his small movements, including his hand movements, along with better hand–eye coordination. This means he can accurately see what he wants and direct his hands to it. He'll start by grasping with both hands, sometimes "trapping" a toy between them rather than gripping it.

Increasing ability From six months, your baby will reach for something without needing to watch his hands to make sure they're on track to get it. Now he will grip toys with his whole hand. At around nine months, he will start to use his thumb and finger to pick things up. As he reaches 12 to 15 months, this pincer grip will become increasingly refined and dextrous.

Hand control

Exploring through taste

Your young explorer has discovered her mouth and she wants to put everything into it. Laden with nerve endings and taste buds, her mouth and tongue give her information on flavor, texture, and consistency.

How these activities help your baby

When you encourage her to discover taste and texture with her mouth, you are helping your baby:

★ Develop hand–eye coordination. She's figuring out the position of her hands in relation to the rest of her body.

★ Get a grip. Each object or piece of food she grasps gives her practice in opening and closing her hand, fingers, and mouth.

★ Move her tongue. Tiny movements of your baby's tongue are needed for speaking and eating—mouthing is great practice for these skills.

★ Investigate. This area of her body is highly sensitive and provides intense feedback to her developing brain.

★ Stimulate her senses. She's finding out about new sensations by experiencing them on her lips and tongue.

Toes to mouth Your baby's body is very flexible. Pop her on her back and she'll touch and grab her feet and even bring them to her mouth. This combination of small and large movements is good practice for more complex coordination later on.

KEY FACT
At birth babies prefer sweet flavors and dislike sour ones. They show no reaction to salty flavors until about four months, when they start to develop a taste for them.

Different feelings Your baby uses her hands, lips, tongue, and mouth to investigate. Offer her a variety of safe objects to bring to her mouth, such as a chilled teething ring, or soft, squashy, or textured toys.

Safe and sound Your baby will put whatever she can, small or large, into her mouth to investigate it thoroughly. Offer only safe objects that are larger than her mouth to avoid choking.

Removing choking hazards

Once your baby starts to put everything in her mouth, you need to be extra vigilant about anything that's within her reach that could pose a choking hazard.

Household dangers Regularly check floors and other surfaces for small items that might present a choking risk. Coins, buttons, paperclips, pen tops, and small batteries are all dangerous to babies and small children. Choose toys that are labeled as safe for babies, since toys for older children can have small parts that she could choke on.

Solid foods When you introduce solid foods, seek advice about which are safe for your baby. Always cut or chop food into very small pieces and supervise babies at mealtimes. Some foods are particularly dangerous; these include grapes, small chunks of cheese or meat, cherry tomatoes, raisins, and sticky candy.

Be prepared Find out what to do if your baby does choke. Get information on local first-aid courses from your library or community center or ask your pediatrician.

First food Being able to steer food to his mouth is an excellent use of your baby's new ability to grasp and move smaller objects. When he's ready, at around six months, give finger foods that are easy to hold, such as bananas. Expect mess—he's bound to miss his mouth sometimes while he's working on his coordination.

Hand control

Picking up, letting go

Your baby is fine-tuning his movements to pick up and let go of objects. This isn't easy since his hands and fingers must move with precision to wrap around an object. Consciously opening his hand to let go will come, with practice, later.

How these activities help your baby

Picking up, holding, and letting toys fall from his grasp are new to your baby. When you let him practice in lots of playful ways, you're helping him:

★ Open his hand. Opening his fingers to let a toy drop is a budding skill that your baby will need more and more as his play grows in complexity.

★ Bring his hands together. Using both hands together gives your baby more scope to pick up what he wants.

In addition to helping his manual dexterity, you are also helping him to:

★ Find out more. Your baby can now hold something securely and explore it with his mouth, or bring it into his eye line to examine.

★ Gain satisfaction. He'll be very pleased with himself when he can pick up his toy and shake it deliberately to make a noise.

★ Learn a sequence. Your baby is learning that picking up and letting go over and over are movements he can put together for a purpose.

1 **Your baby finds** picking up easiest when toys are small enough to fit into her hand, but not into her mouth. Acquiring this skill takes patience. Sit her with support and offer an easy-to-hold toy.

2 **Wait while she opens her hand** and wraps her fingers around the toy. She may bring both of her hands together to enable her to pick up the toy with greater ease.

3 **Let her pick up the toy** and give her time to examine and explore it, allowing her to turn it around in her hands, feel its size and texture, and perhaps bring it to her mouth.

4 **While she is holding the first toy,** offer her a new one. Her ability to let go is only just beginning, but when you offer the replacement toy, she will drop the first one automatically.

Hand control

Passing objects

Using his hands is the cornerstone of so many of your baby's activities. In the coming months, he will move from clasping his hands together in front of his body to figuring out how to pass an object between them.

Hand it over Build on your baby's ability to open his hand with passing games. Take turns passing a toy back and forth between you saying "thanks" as you switch. Or hold a light scarf between you and each take turns to tug it gently.

How these activities help your baby

Whether you are handing your baby a toy, playing a passing game, or encouraging him to pass between his hands, you are helping him to:

★ Get his hands working in unison. Your baby needs both hands to cooperate: as one opens, the other must close over what he's passing.

★ Refine his movements. Using feedback from each movement, your baby is trying to make his next move more accurate. Control of his hands and fingers requires lots of practice at flexing, stretching, grasping, and gripping.

Copy me Sit your baby on your lap and slowly move a toy between your hands and he'll watch what you're doing. Prompt him to copy by saying "You do it." Give him time to imitate even just a part of this action.

Back and forth As his small movements gain control, give him a toy and praise him as he grips it and passes it to his other hand. At first he'll curl his hand around it, but his grip will gradually loosen, making passing easier.

KEY FACT

By this stage your baby can use his pincer grip to pick up and manipulate small and large objects, and pass an object from one hand to the other.

Communication skills

Giggles and rhymes

Your baby is ready to play more interactive games and have fun with words and actions. Introduce her to all your favorite rhyme and movement games and enjoy communicating, laughing, and spending lots of entertaining time together.

How these activities help your baby

When you spend time playing games with words and actions, you are helping your baby:

★ **Take turns.** Good communication relies on taking turns to speak and listen. Games and rhymes make turn-taking fun to learn.

★ **Understand language.** Words and actions together teach the meaning and rhythm of speech.

★ **Wait for something to happen.** The repetition and pauses in games allow your baby to get to know that there is a pattern to communication.

★ **Share her pleasure.** When you are both having fun, your shared emotions enhance the deep bond between you.

TOP TIP
Having fun with your baby provides the right emotional context for her brain to lay down connections between brain cells, paving the way for learning.

Eyes, ears, mouth, and nose Act out rhymes that name parts of her body, pointing to whichever part you're naming. She'll watch with glee. Get her involved by moving her hands to each body part as you say the rhyme more slowly.

Do it again! Your baby will love the repetition of a simple game with words and actions, such as "Itsy-bitsy Spider." Walk your fingers on her as you act out each rhyme and watch her reaction; she'll enjoy each step and anticipate the final tickle.

Share a laugh Surprise your baby by doing something unexpected. Make a face, poke out your tongue, or hide then pop up. Repeat it with a smile and raised eyebrows and she'll read your signals that this is a funny game and will laugh along with you.

How silly! Your baby will be spellbound if you make teddy bears or toys talk to or play act with each other. Use a silly voice for each character and move them as you tell their story, making each act just a minute or two. Repeat this often for a good giggle.

Focusing on your baby

Giving your baby the best start in life is your priority. You may wonder at times about the right way to do this and, like many parents, question whether you're doing a good job. Be reassured that your baby will do well with lots of your time, close attention, and conversation.

Focused attention Research suggests that babies benefit most when parents are focused on them during playtime. Watch and comment on her play regularly, and get involved, rather than simply keeping an eye on her while you do something else.

Plenty of talk Your baby's communication skills will develop quickly when you talk to her every chance you get. Research shows that babies of talkative moms gain a greater vocabulary than children of quieter mothers, so all that talking really can make a difference.

Time with you The range of educational toys and teaching aids for babies, such as baby flashcards and training DVDs, may give you the impression that everyday play and communication isn't enough. However, some studies suggest otherwise. For example, it's been found that babies shown "baby training" DVDs actually have fewer words in their vocabulary than those who have never seen them. What really counts, and gives her the best start in life, is a wide variety of play, speech, and stimulation with her favorite playmates—her family.

(Communication skills)

Walking and talking

Your baby is interested in every word. He's primed to listen and the more you speak, the quicker he'll understand. Describe what he sees when you're on the move. Keep doing this, and he'll be a chatterbox, too!

How these activities help your baby

When you talk as you walk around, you are helping your baby:

★ **Build his vocabulary.** He's not using words yet, but the more you speak, the greater the number of words your baby will use in future.

★ **Listen.** Your tone of voice, gestures and eye contact encourage your baby to listen to what you are saying.

★ **Hold his interest.** Your descriptions make even the most mundane trip out fascinating to your baby.

Keep talking With a backward-facing carriage or stroller, you can easily talk as you walk and watch your baby's reaction. Tell him where you are going and who he will meet. He's getting to know the story of his day.

Nature watch Colors and movement in your yard or at the park will attract his attention. As he turns or babbles, notice what's caught his eye then pause, watch, and describe what he sees. Let him touch the leaves or tree trunk as you tell him about them.

Communication skills

Body language

Your baby's whole body is an instrument for communication. As he waves his fists and legs, arches his back or snuggles forward, turns his head away or stares intently, his face and body tell you how he feels.

Let me sleep Your baby needs up to three naps a day and will tell you he's tired by rubbing his eyes, pulling at his ear, twirling his hair, or rubbing his face. This sends you a message and soothes him, too.

No more Your baby can't say "stop" or "no," but arching back, turning away, closing her eyes, frowning, crying, or flushing all give you that message. Act on these signs and she'll gain confidence that you understand her.

How these activities help your baby

When you tune in to his body language, you are helping your baby:

★ **Tell you what he needs.** The better you are at reading his body signals, the more quickly you can figure out what he wants and respond to him.

★ **Communicate more.** Each time your baby's body language is successful, he's motivated to use these actions again to communicate with you.

★ **Reinforce his messages.** Your baby's expressions and gestures will continue to be important, even once he starts to use words to express himself.

I like it Turning toward you, opening his eyes, kicking his legs, waving his arms, and smiling or squealing are all signals that he likes what is happening and wants you to keep going. Match his expressions with your own to show that you've noticed.

TOP TIP
When your baby starts to show signals of sleepiness, settle him down to sleep so he doesn't end up crying. If you miss his signals and keep playing, he is likely to become overly tired and fussy.

Communication skills

Story time

Entrance, entertain, and educate your baby as you spin a tale that introduces her to new words, colorful pictures and stories that become solid favorites. You are starting her love affair with books and adding to her growing ability to listen and understand.

What's that? Point to and identify the pictures in your baby's board or cloth book. He needs to see the picture and hear the name of an object over and over again to label it and be able to say it in the future.

How these activities help your baby

Whenever you tell a story or show your baby a book, you are helping her:

★ Make out new words. As you repeat her favorite stories, your baby begins to recognize the sound of each word.

★ Pay attention. When she's interested in the story, your baby will naturally practice her listening skills.

★ Get to know what words look like. In order to decipher them later, your baby needs to recognize the shapes of letters and words. This will eventually give her a head start in learning to read.

Family history Stories don't need to be made up. When you tell your baby about your real-life family history, she learns language and hears about her own heritage too. Show her photos and tell her a story about the people, events, and emotions.

Communication skills

Listening and learning

Communication is about listening as well as speaking. Your baby's eyes and ears are open to learn more. She watches your moves, registering the shape of your mouth and your expression, and listens to the sound of your words. Do the same and you're truly communicating.

First sounds Babbling and cooing are your baby's opening attempts to use her voice. Listen carefully and repeat sounds back to her. Hearing this encourages her to repeat the sounds and teaches her turn taking.

Extra information As you talk, exaggerate your expression to help your baby recognize added clues about what you're saying. Lift your eyebrows and tilt your head to signal a question; smile or frown to show emotion.

How these activities help your baby

When you get up close to your baby, speak clearly and listen well, you are helping her:

★ **Form more sounds.** Your baby is learning by watching and copying how you move your mouth to make sounds.

★ **Express herself.** Your feedback tells your baby that her sounds are meaningful to you.

★ **Get into a rhythm.** Your baby is learning the pattern—speak, pause, listen, pause—that is the basis for smooth communication.

Early learning Your baby learns best when you speak to him face to face, close up with a singsong voice. This combination of facial expressions, high-pitched tone, long vowels, and short sentences is called "parentese" and comes naturally to new parents.

KEY FACT
By around six months, you'll notice your baby start putting two sounds together such as "mmm-ahhh." She'll also repeat a sound like "dadadada."

(Communication skills)

Crash, bang!

Your baby loves to make a noise and he'll be sure to grab your attention when he gets his hands on his first musical instruments! At this age, it's all about the pure enjoyment of making sounds and creating a simple beat.

How these activities help your baby

As you make music and noise together, you are helping your baby to:

★ Practice patterns. The beat of music and songs prepares your baby for the rhythms of speech.

★ Wait and listen. As you and your baby take turns making noises, he's having a musical conversation.

★ Love music. You're encouraging him to make and listen to tunes and melody for the sheer pleasure of it.

★ Move his body. He needs to gain good control of his arms and hands to make music.

The beat goes on Your baby can recognize a musical beat a few days after he is born, and by the time he's three months old, wants to make his own version. Offer shakers or a tambourine, then join in or tap out a beat with your hands as he makes a noise.

KEY FACT
In the uterus, your baby can make out sounds from 23 weeks' gestation. Playing music that he heard during your pregnancy will comfort him, since he finds it familiar and soothing.

For the pure joy of it Give your baby access to as much music as you possibly can. Play him CDs, sing to him, and try him with a keyboard, rainmakers, xylophone, and musical play mats. If you play an instrument to him, he's sure to be transfixed.

Shake and make music One of his earliest instruments will be his rattle. At first, he'll be surprised by the noise, turn and wait for more, then discover he can repeat it. He'll love to keep this sequence —of making a noise then listening—going.

Big bangs Your baby just loves to make a loud noise—give him household pans and spoons and he'll create a racket. Join in yourself after he's banged his "drum." This turn-taking reinforces the pattern of communication between you.

Brain power

Imitating you

Your baby is a natural–born mimic. She's arrived ready to copy, and her subject matter is anything she can see, hear, or experience. She'll look to you as her first and most important example—you are her first teacher and copying you is one of her main priorities.

How these activities help your baby

When opportunities to copy come thick and fast, you are helping your baby:

★ Learn quickly and effectively. Copying is an excellent way for her to learn.

★ Develop pathways in her brain. Each time she copies, she's creating new connections or strengthening existing ones between brain cells; this in turn promotes brain development.

★ Gain skills. As your baby copies and repeats over and over, she is refining her abilities and skills.

★ Take turns. The pattern of showing, then copying helps your baby practice turn taking; she will need this for playing games as well as communication.

TOP TIP

Mirrors are great communication tools: by six months, your baby can see his reflection in the mirror and may have conversations with his new "friend."

Funny faces Making a face is an exaggeration of your usual expression and that makes it easier for your baby to copy. Make the face slowly, hold it, and pause for her to copy then repeat. Try sticking out your tongue, smiling, or widening your eyes and raising your eyebrows.

Mouth moves Forming different shapes with her mouth and moving her tongue are important skills in readiness for speech. Hold her facing you, attract her attention then make a shape, such as an "O" with your mouth for her to copy.

Blowing raspberries Around four or five months old, your baby will start making wet "razzing" sounds, often forming bubbles on her lips. Purse your lips to make a "brr-ing" sound with your own mouth for her to copy. This helps with both speaking and eating.

Copycat Your baby is naturally drawn to look at faces. She's laying down pathways in her brain that help her recognize expressions and facial movements. Give her plenty to look at and imitate, then mimic her face back to her so she knows you've seen.

Hands up! His hands and fingers hold a fascination for your baby and he's ready to copy simple movements. Hold up your hand and wiggle your fingers, or clap to see if he will try it too. Do this time and again—he loves the repetition.

Brain power

Visual stimulation

Your baby's eyesight is developing rapidly. He can now focus with greater accuracy, and by four months sees more detail and color. His eyesight isn't as good as yours, but he'll learn a lot through looking.

How these activities help your baby

By giving your baby a rich variety of things to see, you are helping him:

★ **Develop his brain.** He uses feedback from what he sees to understand and respond to his world and to move around.

★ **Gain depth perception.** He is developing his ability to see in three dimensions; he needs rich, interesting, visual scenery to do this.

★ **Focus on a moving object.** It takes practice, muscle control, and both eyes working together to track a moving object.

★ **Copy.** His most effective learning comes through watching and copying.

Near and far The outdoors is ideal for your baby to work on depth perception. As she focuses on things that are close or far away, such as birds, branches, and flowers, she is giving her brain information that enhances her ability to see in three dimensions.

Absorbing Your baby is taking in information about color, shape, and size. Give her toys that reflect these different properties, such as brightly colored toys, shaped blocks, and balls of various sizes. She'll explore them with her eyes as well as her hands.

Role model You and your partner are the most important people in your baby's life and everything you do will be interesting to him. Let him watch as you do your daily tasks. Pop him in his chair to see you cook, or on a nearby rug when you are doing laundry.

Watch it move Help your baby's eyes work well together by moving your fingers or a toy, or dancing a puppet slowly, across his line of vision. As he gets steadily better at tracking an object, you can gradually move a little faster.

As the world goes by As your baby grows, a forward-facing stroller gives him a great view of his surroundings. Facing outward in an upright position, he can constantly take in colors, movement, and shapes as he cruises by.

Good viewpoint Your baby will be relaxed and able to concentrate on what he can see when he views the world from the safety of your arms or held close in a forward-facing baby carrier while you move around your home or go for a walk outside.

A change of scenery

Your baby is intensely curious to see the world around him and will learn something from every new environment you offer him.

Everyday sights Your baby will be at his most comfortable when exploring at home with you nearby to keep him company. Each room is packed full of things for him to look at and learn about, from his toys and teddy bears to your pots and pans, patterns on the rug, pictures and mirrors on the wall, and the view from the window.

Looking at nature In your yard or local park, your baby's senses will be stimulated by the movement of trees and leaves, dogs and squirrels, natural colors, and the opportunity to adjust his eyes to look into the distance and close up. Studies have shown that babies tend to sleep better at night the more daylight and fresh air they are exposed to. You will benefit too, since evidence suggests that being in a natural environment improves your sense of well-being.

Different environments The bright colors and lights of a large supermarket may overly stimulate your baby, but a quick visit to the local stores is just right to take in the view of shelves and shapes.

Brain power

The art of anticipation

She's ready, waiting, and excited about what comes next. Your baby's memory is developing, and with it her ability to predict your next move and get worked up about it. Her reaction tells you whether or not she wants that tickle, drink, or bath: she's making her preferences known.

How these activities help your baby

By repeating games and routines and making her life predictable you are helping your baby:

★ **Remember.** Daily routines and repetitive play allow your baby to build up her memory.

★ **Learn to wait.** She won't hold on for long, but your baby is finding out that she can deal with waiting.

★ **Figure out what she likes.** Her improving memory allows your baby to compare foods, drinks, toys, and games.

You are also helping her:

★ **Feel safe and secure.** Being able to predict what will happen next builds your baby's sense of security.

Reach out Your baby anticipates the pleasure of a hug and can signal she wants one. When you read and react to her gestures, hugging as she reaches out or offering a toy she's staring at, you strengthen her expectations that her needs will be met.

TOP TIP
At this age your baby won't be able to remember what you told her she could or couldn't do for very long: be ready to repeat yourself time and time again.

Getting excited Her ability to remember is clear when she gets excited waiting for something she likes. Build her expectations. Say "Do you want this?" and smile and widen your eyes to emphasize the question.

What's next? Your baby needs to know what comes next. Teach him what to expect by telling him what's happening next. Explain one thing at a time: "It's bathtime" or "I'm getting your drink" and repeat it each time.

Wait for it When a game has a big ending, such as bouncing, tipping, or tickling, hold off for a few seconds before the last move to build excitement. This gives your baby the experience of delay and shows her that waiting will be rewarded.

Making memories

Your baby can recognize your face, anticipate what comes next in her favorite rhyme, and has learned that when she reaches out her arms you will pick her up. There's a clear progression in her memory development.

Quick progression Your baby's ability to remember develops rapidly. Research suggests that a baby's ability to retain information doubles between the ages of three and six months.

Types of memory Over her first year, your baby is developing her working memory, which holds information for a few seconds, and her long-term memory, where information is stored and can be recalled. Memory development depends on the gradual maturing of your baby's brain and so this cannot be rushed.

Repetition and focus What she can remember depends on a couple of important factors. Repetition is incredibly important to your baby. The more often she sees, hears, or experiences something, the better chance she has of remembering it. The other important aspect in your baby's development of memory is her ability to pay attention. The more she focuses her attention on something, the better she will hold it in her working memory.

Brain power

Yes and no

Your baby is preparing to understand some big ideas, including the concepts of "yes" and "no." This is your first attempt to guide him. He won't begin to understand the concept of "no" until he's at least six months old.

How these activities help your baby

When you say "yes" as you encourage your baby and "no" as you stop him, you are helping him:

★ **Gain awareness of these key concepts.** Linking words, gestures, and actions teaches your baby the meaning of "yes" and "no."

★ **Begin to understand instructions.** As you pair the word "no" with an action, such as holding your baby back from touching something hot, you teach him that the word means he should stop.

★ **Tune in.** Your baby is primed to please you and wants to know what gets your approval. "Yes" and "no" become clear signals of what you do and don't want him to do.

Keep going Your baby will look to you for encouragement, and later for permission, for what he is doing. Say "yes" at every opportunity and pair it with a nodding head and smile. This is a powerful combination to convey your message.

Oh no you don't At this age, you'll want to stop your baby if he gets too close to a hazard, and start to teach him that some actions are wrong. Pair this with a clear shake of the finger and say "no" in a firm tone so he links stopping to the gesture and word.

KEY FACT
Baby babble is the same the world over; it's only when babies learn to use words in any given language that they discard the sounds that they don't need.

Practicing "no" Your baby is learning the concept of "no" by copying your gestures. As you read out loud, or play with puppets, pause when there's a "no" in the story and do a head or finger shake and small frown for him to copy.

How necessary is discipline?

Your baby is learning quickly and is motivated above all else by your loving approval.

Baby behavior Your baby doesn't yet appreciate that some of his cries and actions could upset or irritate you. Equally, he's into everything out of curiosity and the drive to explore, rather than because he's deliberately being naughty.

Here and now Even if you do say "no" to your three- to six-month-old baby, he won't be able to remember the specifics for the next time because his long-term memory is not yet well-enough developed. As a result, there is no need for discipline strategies at this young age.

Positive reinforcement Your most effective tool to guide your baby is to give attention and praise and show your pleasure when he does something you like or want him to keep doing. This will usually come naturally since you will be so delighted with his achievements, perhaps when he's tried a finger food, begun to babble, or rolled over. You'll automatically reward him with a beaming smile, praise, and a hug.

Brain power

Fuel your baby's senses

The world is full of noise, smells, tastes, sights, and textures, and your baby is having an exciting time discovering it with you. Revive your own senses as you offer your baby her first smell of a flower, a taste of a banana, or a listen to one of your favorite pieces of music.

How these activities help your baby

When you give your baby plenty to excite her senses you are helping to:

★ **Feed her brain.** All of her senses pass information to her brain to be put together to build up her knowledge of the world.

★ **Understand that she has several senses.** At birth, your baby cannot clearly separate her senses; she has to work on deciphering which is which.

★ **Tolerate new sensations.** At first your baby will startle easily. As her senses mature, she will gradually manage more noise and stronger light, smells, and tastes.

★ **Develop preferences.** As she discovers different sensations, your baby will find those she enjoys or dislikes.

TOP TIP
Your baby can now distinguish colors almost as well as adults do. Stimulate her vision with walks to the park or stores, or a couple of hours at the zoo.

Treasure basket Stimulate your baby with a bowl of household objects of different shapes and textures. Include a wooden spoon, citrus fruit, fabrics, noisy toys, and plastic containers. Change the items regularly to hold her interest.

Fragrant flora There is plenty to bombard your baby's senses outdoors. Hold him close to a fragrant flower or blossom and let him smell and look at it. His senses will be fully engaged and he may even notice how the scene changes as shadows move across it.

Blowing in the wind Your baby's attention will be drawn to bright colors as well as movement. Captivate him with the sight of a whirling windmill—he'll be fascinated by the effect of the wind on the sails and the blur of color that results.

Tasty treats Everything your baby picks up finds its way into her mouth, and by six months she'll be trying finger foods. Start her off with only one new taste at a time and keep it fairly bland. Her taste buds need time to adjust to each new flavor.

Hear the difference Your baby is learning to hear various tones. Offer him toys that rattle and jingle, and make deep and high noises. Let him hear one noise and give him time to listen, wait then make another. He can consider and compare what he hears.

How the senses develop

Over time, your baby's senses become more acute, enabling her to take in more information about her world.

Sensory jumble At first, the pathways for the senses in your baby's brain aren't separated out. This combining of her senses is called "synaethesia," where two or more senses are mixed. For example, a baby may hear a sound and see it as a color or as a visual disturbance. It's still not clear when the senses separate out: some experts say around two to four months, while others suggest this happens later.

Hearing and sight At birth, your baby's hearing is more highly developed than her sight. By six months, she will turn toward your voice, even at a distance. Improving her focus, perception of shades and colors, and tracking of moving objects is a priority in your baby's first months. By eight months, her sight is almost as good as it will be in adulthood.

Taste Your baby is born with a preference for sweet tastes over salty; this is in readiness for the sweet taste of breast milk. She has more taste buds than later in life and is sensitive to strong flavors.

Smell This develops rapidly: she recognizes the smell of your breast milk compared to that of another mother's at a few days old.

Touch Your baby explores through touch in her early days. This sense really advances once her reflexes fade, at around three months of age.

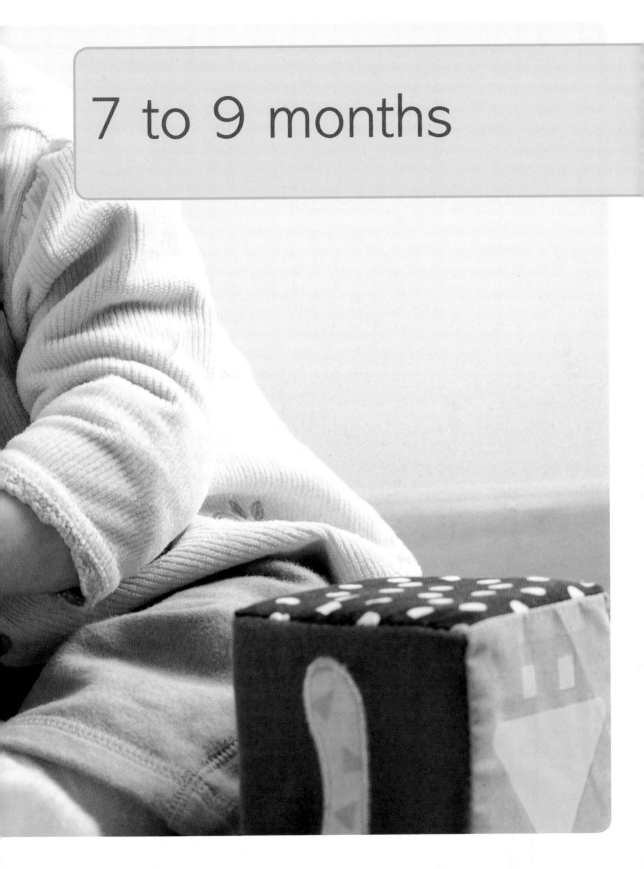

7 to 9 months

YOUR MOVING BABY

Your baby's increased coordination and her improved understanding of her environment mean that she is truly beginning to take more control over her activities. Her world of play opens up as she begins to understand some key concepts.

YOUR SOCIAL BABY

Your baby's self awareness is growing and with this comes the realization that you and she are separate—if she can't see you, this means that you're not there! No matter how nurturing and reassuring you are, at around eight months, she'll start to experience separation anxiety: she'll show you in no uncertain terms how unhappy she is when you leave her, even if just for a moment, but will quickly calm when you return. This can be distressing for you both, but it's a normal stage of social development and can last until your child is around three years of age!

Over the coming months, she'll learn about a complex range of emotions, from joy and love to anger and frustration. She may also start to show more of an interest in other babies and try to make contact by patting, touching, and babbling to them. However, interactive play with her peers is still a long way off.

GETTING MOVING

As your baby's strength and muscle control continue to develop, she faces the challenge of coordinating different parts of her body so that she can make complex movements. Her next mobility milestone is crawling, which may not appear too demanding, but when you look closer, your baby must multitask: she's holding herself up on hands and knees while also moving each arm and leg alternately to get that forward motion.

Once she is confident crawling, she may start to pull herself up onto furniture to stand—a totally new experience for her.

HAND CONTROL

Your baby's fine motor control continues to improve and is a major step in her command of her environment. Managing the muscles in her hands and coordinating movements to aim for something she can see give her the essential skills she needs to reach, pick up, and manipulate small objects. These skills are helped once she masters coordination in the rest of her body. Gaining some command of her bigger muscles helps to create a stable base from which she can manage the smaller movements of her arms and hands to reach and grab. The ability to sit up securely, at around six to seven months, gives her this firm base, enabling her to direct her hands.

From six to nine months, she'll perfect the ability to pass toys between her hands. She will also reach for something she can see without watching her hands to make sure they're on track to get it.

Getting stronger Your baby will enjoy being supported by you as she practices new, more challenging movements.

Clever me Mastering the coordination needed to bring both of her hands together to clap will delight your baby.

Hold it steady Your baby has the muscle control in her hands and fingers to hold a book still while she looks at the pictures.

Crawling Between six and 12 months, most babies learn to crawl—although some move in other ways, such as bottom shuffling, and skip this stage. Whether or not your baby crawls, floor level activities are important to keep her on the move.

COMMUNICATION SKILLS

At around seven to nine months, your baby will be eager to copy the sounds that you make. Her comprehension is also improving, and at around the same time, she may understand when you say "bye bye" or "no." The more you communicate with your baby by touch, look, gesture, singing, and speaking, the better her language development. So don't be embarrassed to give her a running commentary on whatever she can see, or to sing and chatter to her throughout the day; never fear—she'll love your rhymes and lullabys, whether or not you're in tune!

Along with her spoken communication, your baby is learning how to use gestures to let you know what she means. These movements, which start to appear around six months as she gains arm and hand control, give you extra information to help you understand what she wants. For example, she'll show she's ready to be picked up by reaching out with her arms and, at around nine months, she'll clap her hands to show delight and will begin to point—a skill that significantly increases her ability to communicate with you.

BRAIN POWER

Your baby's understanding of the concept of cause and effect will continue to grow during this period and will feature strongly in her play. At around the same time, she will also figure out that things still exist even when she can't see them. This major cognitive development is known as object permanence and is vital to your baby's understanding of how the world works. You'll notice it when you play peekaboo or see her search for a hidden toy, knowing it is there somewhere.

Sharing experiences Talking about everything you see enhances your communication with your baby.

Your social baby

Reassuring your baby

Suddenly, your baby doesn't want you out of her sight: this is the start of separation anxiety. Her awareness has increased and she's not sure when you'll be back. This starts at around eight months and may last up to three years.

How these activities help your baby

When you work hard to make separation less upsetting for your baby, you are helping her:

★ **Be less stressed.** If your baby is left with familiar, comforting people, she'll manage better.

★ **Begin to soothe herself.** As she uses toys and blankets for comfort, your baby is learning she can calm herself.

★ **Build her confidence.** When you start with only short separations, your baby begins to realize you will always come back.

★ **Lower her anxiety.** Always say a warm goodbye, or your baby will worry that you may leave her any time.

Don't go Being apart from you is hard for your baby, so start with only short separations of five to ten minutes to build up her confidence that you always come back to her. Leave her only with people you trust to comfort her.

Introductions Always leave your baby with someone she knows. Introduce her to babysitters or caregivers in advance, and let your baby look at the new person while she is snuggled in your arms before you pass her over for a first hug.

TOP TIP
Try not to leave your baby when she is likely to be tired, hungry, or restless. If at all possible, schedule your departures for after naps and mealtimes.

Comfort blanket When you are away, your baby may want to hold and suck her comfort toy or something that smells of you, perhaps clothing you have worn. The sight, feel and scent will soothe her.

Welcome back Make each reunion with your baby a big deal. Greet her with hugs, strokes, eye contact, and big smiles before you turn to her babysitter or caregiver to ask how she's been.

Your social baby

Becoming assertive

Your baby has personality and plenty of it now. She's beginning to demonstrate her emotions more clearly, signaling her likes and dislikes and showing her determination to learn. As she reveals more of her character, enjoy this new phase of getting to know her.

How these activities help your baby

When you encourage your baby to express herself and show her personality you are helping her:

★ Develop her character. Your baby will thrive on your acceptance of her personality and preferences.

★ Handle strong emotions. Your soothing presence, calm words, and touch can help your baby deal with strong feelings.

★ Keep trying. You'll use both encouragement and distraction to help your baby through the frustration of learning something new.

Stop doing that As she tries out new behaviors, your baby sometimes needs to be told "no." Use the word firmly and patiently as you stop her; she's only just beginning to learn there are limits.

Expressing herself As a storm of emotion triggers your baby to yell and kick, cry or fuss, help her handle it by staying calm yourself: name the feeling she's expressing and reassure her with touch as she quiets down.

Your social baby

Shyness with strangers

Your "smile at anyone" baby has turned shy. It's all part of separation anxiety and doesn't mean he'll always be this way. Introduce him gently to new people and places: he'll need your help to be sociable.

How these activities help your baby

By gently introducing him to anyone new and tuning in to his reaction you are helping him:

★ Handle new situations. Knowing you are there and will take things at his pace gives him confidence to be social.

★ Practice his social skills. He will bring out his friendly smile and babbles once he is comfortable.

★ Build his social network. Being social yourself helps your baby socialize—you are his role model and your confidence will rub off on him.

★ Use you as his safe base. He's able to meet other children because he knows he can always come back to you.

Hold him tight In any new situation, your baby wants your reassurance and he'll press himself into you for maximum comfort. Respond by holding him close; as he gradually relaxes, he may risk peeking out and looking around.

KEY FACT

At this age, your baby is interested in other babies. He doesn't want to play together yet since he's too busy developing his own skills, but may want to touch, smile, and babble.

No rush Let your baby take his time getting to know someone new. He'll start by gazing, and then may smile, babble, or coo as he feels more at ease. It may take a few visits for him to relax with someone new.

Slow and easy does it Your baby will be happier to meet new people when they approach slowly, use a gentle tone of voice and don't crowd him. Tune in to his reaction so you know when he's had enough.

Increasing confidence The more social you are, the more practice your baby has being with others. Parent and baby groups, seeing friends, or taking baby swimming or massage all help him to socialize.

Getting moving

Sitting comfortably

Your baby is strong enough to sit securely. This means she has the stability and strength to perfect big and small movements. Share her triumph as she pushes her balance to the limit to grab a toy or reach out for you.

How these activities help your baby

When you keep her entertained as she sits without support, you're helping her:

★ **Grow stronger.** You may not see much movement, but her leg and trunk muscles are working hard to keep her body balanced.

★ **Coordinate her body.** To sit and play without wobbling, your baby must get all of her muscle groups working smoothly together.

★ **Reach and stretch with confidence.** A stable sitting position allows your baby to do so much more now with her arms and hands.

Sit up Sit on the floor with your baby and surround her with toys that she can explore. Try holding them up so she must reach upward and outward to grab them. She's working on her balance and becoming more stable in the process.

Hold it As your baby masters the art of sitting, she will be able to stay still and concentrate on what's in her hands. Give her books, toys, and blocks to hold and explore. Put a toy out in front or to the side to encourage her to pivot forward or lean sideways.

Pulling up

It is one skill to pull up to stand and quite another to get back down. Your baby's pride in getting up will take a tumble as she lands back down, her body a little out of control. Don't worry though—with a little help from you, she'll soon master getting back down, too.

Pull up Encourage your baby to stand as she grabs the top of her crib, your knees or the edge of the sofa or coffee table to raise herself. Motivate her by putting out toys that she can only reach by standing.

Guiding hand It's so much easier for your baby to stand up than to guide her body back down again. Steady her by holding both her hands so she can bend her knees to squat as she sits.

How these activities help your baby

When you give your baby opportunities to practice pulling up and sitting down, you are helping her:

★ **Learn to squat down.** The strength and coordination to make this move takes lots of practice.

★ **Have a safe landing.** Your baby will be confident to pull up if she knows falling won't be so bad.

★ **Pull up with confidence.** Stronger legs and better balance make your baby steadier on her feet.

Soft landing There's a lot of trial and error as your baby works on pulling up to stand. He's bound to fall, so place cushions or a rug for a soft landing. Make sure he's not practicing near dangers such as a fireplace.

Easy does it By holding your baby's waist as she sits down, you keep her body steady and upright. You are guiding her through the right body positions to go from standing to sitting and this will help her do it herself.

KEY FACT

As your baby's ability to use the furniture for support improves, she may "cruise" around it. In a few weeks, she may let go completely and stand alone for a few moments.

Getting moving

Encouraging mobility

Whether he rolls, wiggles, or has started to crawl, your baby is on the move. You'll be amazed at how quickly he gets around. Double check the babyproofing and watch him like a hawk—he's getting into everything.

How these activities help your baby

When you give him plenty to explore and lots of space to move you are helping your baby:

★ Progress from a wiggle to a crawl. Each stage of mobility, from rolling to being on his hands and knees, brings your baby closer to crawling.

★ Coordinate his legs and arms. To crawl effectively, he must move his opposite arm and leg at the same time. Play time on the floor is his best place to practice.

★ Move no matter what. Your baby may not crawl or even bottom shuffle to be mobile; some babies miss out this stage and go on to walk without crawling at all.

Into everything Once your baby can move from sitting on to her hands and knees, she's perfectly positioned to crawl and will be motivated to explore. Set up plastic bowls, cups, and spoons in a low cupboard for her to play with, or a basket of soft toys to discover.

Floor time Introduce floor-level activities to get your baby moving. He may rock back and forth on his knees, shuffle, or crawl. A mat with noises, lights, and things to grab; pop-up toys; push-and-go cars; and baby play centers will all appeal to him.

KEY FACT

If you are thinking of putting your baby into a "sit in" baby walker, familiarize yourself with the safety issues—this equipment has a high accident rate and is banned in some countries.

Obstacle course Challenge your baby's new-found mobility by giving him a baby nest to climb into, or pillows or cushions on the floor to squirm over or roll off. Or drape a sheet over the kitchen table to create a tunnel to crawl through.

Bottom shuffles Not every baby crawls —for some, bottom shuffling is an effective way to move. If your baby bottom shuffles, he may walk a little later, but this is nothing to worry about. Continue encouraging him to move this way and he'll get around well.

Move together Get down on the floor on your hands and knees with your baby and practice crawling together. Your baby will try to copy you, and you will get a child's view of your home and find out just what a challenge crawling can be.

Mobility milestones

Babies vary in the rate they develop, with some reaching major milestones earlier than expected, while others do things in their own time.

What's normal? Most parents ask themselves at some point "Is my baby developing normally?" However, there isn't a straightforward answer to this and it's important to be aware that developmental milestones are only a guide to the time most babies reach a stage. For example, about half of children begin to walk by the age of one, but health professionals would only show concern if your baby still wasn't walking by the time he was 18 months old.

A desire to move Individual babies may reach milestones in a different order, or miss out a stage entirely. With mobility, as long as your baby shows an interest in reaching toys, and eventually moving around, then it doesn't matter how he achieves this. If he bottom shuffles and shows no interest in crawling, it means he's found his own way to get around and is developing fine.

Getting advice If you're concerned, check with your parents and your partner's parents since "late" walking runs in families. Or ask questions at your baby's regular checkups. If your baby is not reaching his milestones or has areas of difficulty, make an appointment with your doctor to check this out. The chances are you will be reassured, but if there's a problem, the sooner you get help the better, because early intervention is known to get the best results.

Clap hands

Your baby is mastering the complicated movement that is clapping. Her arms and hands are working together: she can open and flatten her palms and make the rapid, smooth movements summed up as a clap.

How these activities help your baby

As you play games and say rhymes that involve clapping you're helping her:

★ **Fine tune her movements.** Clapping involves a quick and complex set of movements, and it takes practice to bring them all together.

★ **Move to the beat.** Timing of movements is essential to clapping. Moving to a rhyme or beat can help.

★ **Coordinate eye and hand.** The accuracy of your baby's movements depends on her ability to match them to what she's seeing.

Hands together Actively teach your baby the complicated set of arm and hand movements needed for clapping. Softly clap your hands first, then gently put them over his and bring them together. Add a rhyme to give rhythm to the clapping.

Hands in front Practice the faster moves of clapping by passing or rolling a soft ball to your baby so he must bring both hands together to the middle of his body in order to trap it.

Patty-cake By nine months, your baby may be able to clap along to rhymes such as "Patty-cake." Say them slowly and put your hands out for her to pat. Clapping to a beat makes these repetitive movements easier.

Clap happy The big, generous movements of clapping reflect how your baby is feeling. Play action games such as "If you're happy and you know it" and clap to show you are happy. She'll watch you and enjoy the movement, and will recognize that it can have meaning.

Hand control

Holding and exploring

Your baby is gaining control over his wrist, hands, and fingers. He can pick up objects between finger and thumb, then twist, turn, and pass them between his hands as he investigates their shape and size.

How these activities help your baby

When you offer toys to keep your baby's hands and fingers busy, you are helping your baby:

★ Bring his thumb and finger together. This "pincer" grasp is one of his most valuable skills, allowing your baby to pick up small objects.

★ Coordinate wrist and hand movements. Being able to rotate his wrist means your baby can turn objects in his hand and explore their shape, size and texture fully.

★ Give and take. Being able to let go is a developing skill, and your baby practices every time he passes an object between his hands.

Turn the page Your baby is starting to bring his finger and thumb together into a pincer grasp to turn the pages of his books. He'll find thick board books and plastic bath books with just a few stiff pages the easiest to practice on.

Twist and turn Using his wrist, hand, and fingers to grip and twist, your baby can work a baby steering wheel or activity center with knobs and dials to press and turn. He'll want to practice on real-life objects, such as the door handle, too.

TOP TIP

Your baby's fine motor control skills are improving. In addition to holding, passing, exploring, and dropping, he may also be able to manage a two-handled sippy cup.

Hand to hand Your baby has mastered the art of opening and closing her grip to pass objects between her hands. Start by passing her an easily held toy, then guide her to pass the toy between her hands. She'll learn quickly to do this herself.

Pop it in Using her pincer grasp and hand–eye coordination while playing with shape sorters, post-it toys, or helping you put a letter in the mailbox, all give your baby a thrill as she watches things disappear from sight.

Hand control

Messy mealtimes

What a mess! Your baby is learning to bring food to his mouth but it's a hit-and-miss affair. He's got a lot to learn: between gripping, lifting the food, then closing his lips around it, he needs coordination and an accurate aim. Be ready for a clean up every time.

I can feed myself Offer your baby finger foods and he'll delight in picking them up and guiding them into his mouth. Don't overwhelm him—put one food at a time on the high-chair tray for him to look at, touch, and grasp.

How these activities help your baby

When you offer him finger foods or a spoon to hold, you are helping him:

★ Grip and grasp. Finger foods provide your baby with practice for his palm and pincer grip.

★ Aim with care. He's been putting things in his mouth for months, but now your baby is directing his movements more precisely.

★ Get feedback. Your baby can't yet control whether his grip is tight or loose, but feedback from his palm and fingers to his brain helps with this fine tuning as the months go by.

Squish, squash Your baby is still practicing how hard to grip, so squashed food in his hand is unavoidable. He's fine tuning the strength of his grasp while enjoying the sensation of mashing food in his fingers.

(Communication skills)

First conversations

Your baby is using an ever widening range of sounds to communicate. As always, she learns by watching, listening, and copying you. Give her a variety of sounds and expressions and she'll start imitating them.

How these activities help your baby

When you hold "conversations" with your baby and respond to her sounds, you are helping her:

★ **Develop her speech.** Copying sounds is a great learning tool for your baby.

★ **Use her lips and tongue to make sounds.** By imitating you, your baby tries out the mouth shapes and tongue positions that form different sounds.

★ **Practice facial expressions.** A lot of information is passed nonverbally by expression and body language. Your baby needs to learn these to boost her communication skills.

Speak and reply Hold a babbling conversation with your baby. Sit up close, face to face, and say a sound or word, then wait for her to babble or "ooh" in return. Keep speaking and listening so she can practice forming sounds and taking turns.

Sound it out Play a copying game with your baby. Look into her face and say "ba" or make a noise such as "brrr." Repeat again and again. When she babbles, say back what she "said" or show your excitement to hear her speak.

Watch my face Your baby is learning about facial expressions as well as sounds. While you read a story or speak to her, make sure she has a good view of your expression. If she mirrors your raised eyebrows, frown, or smile then nod your encouragement.

KEY FACT

At seven or eight months, your baby is not only able to hold conversations with you, she may also mirror your emotions, crying if she sees you cry, for example.

Communication skills

Learning words

Your baby hangs on every word you say, her brain working overtime to understand and remember words. No matter how silly you feel, your running commentary on the world means a lot to her developing speech.

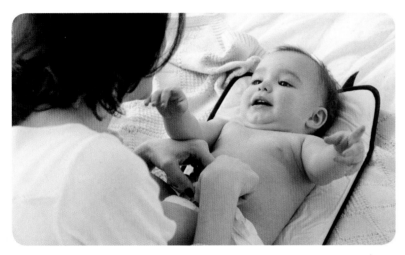

Try "parentese" When you talk to your baby, use exaggerated singsong speech, with short sentences and repetition. This is "parentese," or child-directed speech, and studies show that it helps her pay attention and learn language more quickly.

How these activities help your baby

When you talk, describe, and read to your baby you are helping her:

★ **Build her vocabulary.** The more words she hears, especially repeated time and again, the more she will learn.

★ **Understand language.** From your descriptions, your baby is learning the meaning of words as well as how to make their sounds.

★ **Know what to do.** Your baby is close to the point where she can follow a simple two-word instruction, like "clap hands."

★ **Learn the rules of communication.** She's listening to how sentences, tones and pauses make up speech.

Name it Out and about there is so much to name and describe. Teach your baby real words when you say what you see, rather than shortened or made up names; for example say "banana" rather than "nana" and "dog" rather than "woof woof."

Running commentary You'll never be at a loss for words if you give a running account of everything. With each activity, describe what your baby is doing, the color and shape of toys, and the sounds you can hear.

(Communication skills)

Pointing it out

Your baby is figuring out that aiming his index finger is a powerful communication tool. By nine months, he's beginning to point and make sounds to get your attention and tell you what he wants.

How these activities help your baby

As you show him how to point and then react when he does, you are helping your baby:

★ Figure out the value of gestures. Your baby is learning that pointing is a movement with meaning.

★ Communicate without speaking. Gestures like pointing allow your baby to communicate thoughts such as "look there," then "get it," and "put it here" before he can say what he means.

★ Match words and gestures. When you speak and gesture together, your baby learns that words and actions complement each other.

There it is Your baby is learning that he can direct your attention to an object when he points. Reward him by looking toward and describing what he has pointed to. Point to it or touch it yourself to reinforce using the gesture.

TOP TIP

Pointing to what he wants is an excellent pretalking skill. Follow your baby's finger and show him you understand by saying "You want Teddy?" or "Ben wants another block?".

1 **By nine months,** your baby will be getting the hang of pointing and will love your reaction to it. As he points, ask him "Do you want it?" Copy him by pointing to the object yourself as you say the words to him.

2 **Once you've encouraged him** with praise, smiles, and looking where he points, respond by giving him the object to help him link his gesture and what it means. He'll use pointing to mean "Give me this" by about 15 months.

Communication skills

Move to the music

Add music and movement to words and your baby will learn the tempo and pattern of speech along with the vocabulary. Introduce tunes and rhymes from your own childhood as well as learning new ones together.

Action rhymes The rhythm of a simple verse like "Row the boat" helps your baby learn. Match words with actions. As he goes back and forth, each word will be highlighted by a movement, helping him to remember it.

Dance with me Like speech, music and singing have a pace or tempo. Help your baby experience this by guiding her to move to music. Hold her securely in your arms and sway, jiggle, or gently twirl to the music.

How these activities help your baby

By including music, song, and dance in play time you are helping your baby:

★ Learn by repetition. Favorite verses, jingles, and songs played, sung, or said many times boost your baby's vocabulary.

★ Find the beat in music and language. Spoken sentences rise and fall in tone and pitch like music—hearing one helps your baby learn about the other.

★ Have fun with words and movement. Silly rhymes, simple actions, and funny dance moves will make learning language fun.

Nursery rhyme time Your baby's favorite rhymes are vocabulary builders. As you sing a rhyme like "The wheels on the bus," the same words are repeated, building up familiarity, while each line helps him with the structure of speech.

TOP TIP

If your nursery rhyme repetoire is a bit thin, invest in a DVD for plenty of ideas for rhymes and actions. These are inexpensive and will provide years, of fun for your baby.

Gestures and signs

Your baby communicates her emotion and motivation with increasingly clear expressions and signals. Your challenge is to interpret her gestures and looks and act on them to show her she's understood.

How these activities help your baby

When you interpret and act on her signals, you are helping your baby:

★ **Express herself.** Your baby's face and body give a powerful message as her gestures become more complex.

★ **Build her communication skills.** Gestures and body language add meaning to the spoken word. She will continue using these signals as her speech develops.

★ **Show you how she feels.** When you put a name to her emotions, you are beginning to help your baby label different feelings.

KEY FACT
Around now, when presented with something new, your baby will look to your expression and body language to judge if a situation is safe.

I want to tell you Your baby can't name her feelings, but will communicate them through body language. Turning her head, wrinkling her nose, and tightening her lips may indicate anger, uncertainty, or frustration. Name her emotion as you see it.

Family favorites You're already passing on your gestures to your baby because she sees you do them so often. Pair a sign with an action and she'll quickly figure out the meaning. Rub your tummy as you offer food or show thumbs up when you smile your approval.

Different meanings? Gestures change their meaning depending on what other signals your baby gives. For example, if she smiles at you when she drops a toy, she's saying "This is a game," but with a frown or cry, she is saying "I don't want this."

Baby signing

Baby signing involves hand gestures to represent a word or idea and can be taught from about six months of age.

Why baby sign? Baby signing practitioners report the program allows your baby to express herself earlier and so avoid frustration. For example, she can tell you she wants a drink by making the sign for "milk."

What to consider There's debate about the value of signing. Gestures, expressions, and speech are important in parent–child interaction and occur naturally. Focusing on learned hand movements is of concern to a sizeable group of speech and language therapists. Many advise that the frequent use of natural gestures and good-quality interaction is the ideal for speech and language development. If you do baby sign, include it as an additional area of learning and don't let it take priority over normal gestures, touch, speech, and song. If your baby has delayed speech and language development, maybe because of hearing difficulties, sign language can be a valuable addition to be discussed with a doctor.

I'm signing Learning signs, for what she wants may help your baby communicate simple needs.

(Brain power)

Cause and effect

When your baby discovers that his action causes something to light up, make a sound, or fall over, he'll be delighted and want to do it again. With all the fun, he's grasping a key concept about how the world operates.

How these activities help your baby

When you give your baby toys with lights and bells that react to his actions you are helping him:

★ Understand cause and effect. He's developing the idea that one thing can affect another.

★ Experience how things work. Even though he's not ready to understand the theory, your baby is seeing the effect of gravity, weight, and speed in his play.

★ Gain satisfaction. Each time your baby makes something happen, he receives feedback that he's effective, and this keeps him trying and experimenting.

Knock it down Your baby sees cause and effect in glorious action when she knocks things over. Whether it's a tower of stacking cups or soft blocks, she'll squeal with pleasure as she swipe and topples them.

Pull and roll For every action, your baby will be pleased to see a reaction. Pull-along toys will engage him as he masters control of their direction. He'll enjoy rolling a ball to you too, and watch as you roll it back.

TOP TIP
Good cause and effect toys include mobiles, rattles, stacking toys, pop-up toys, musical toys, pouring cups and squirting toys for the bath, and squeezy toys.

Push up, fall down The effect of gravity adds a wow factor to your baby's actions. He'll enjoy the result of his play when he pushes his car up a ramp then watches it roll down.

Press Whether he's pressing the doorbell or a panel on his toy, your baby is finding out how buttons, knobs, and levers make things happen. Provide toys that beep or light up as he presses, pulls, or pushes them.

Brain power

Out and about

Your baby is alert and ready to notice his environment. He's eager for new sensations and the great outdoors offers him fresh air, a different perspective, and new sounds and sights to stimulate his senses.

Expand her horizon Change your baby's environment to stimulate her senses. Seeing into the distance, feeling the wind on her skin, and noticing changes in the light all offer her senses new information.

How these activities help your baby

When you give your baby time to look at, touch, and enjoy the world outside your home, you are helping him:

★ Explore the elements. Each new environment offers him different smells, textures, and materials to feed his developing senses.

★ Become familiar with different sensations. Your baby is building knowledge of his surroundings on the basis of experience.

★ Enjoy a change of scene. A fresh environment gives him motivation to investigate.

Look and touch The textures, irregular shapes, and variety of practices in the natural environment are all valuable to your baby's sensory development. Give him time to look at and touch the bark of a tree, shells on a beach, or smooth stones by a path.

New experiences So much that is ordinary to you is exciting to your baby. Give him opportunities to watch and listen when you are out. Visit the duck pond, see a boat on the river, a train whizz by, or watch squirrels and birds feed in your yard or the park.

Brain power

Playing peekaboo

It's a major milestone in understanding: your baby is realizing that toys, and you, still exist when she can't see, hear, or touch them. Her grasp of this concept allows her to imagine where a toy is, and play with it in more complex ways.

How these activities help your child

Playing games of search and find, watch and wait, or peekaboo help her:

★ Reinforce her understanding. Your baby is learning through experience that people and things exist whether or not she sees them.

★ Hold people and objects in her mind. It is important to her cognitive development that she can form a mental picture of what is in her world.

★ Develop her memory. These peekaboo games use her visual memory, as she holds an image of the object she's waiting to see.

KEY FACT
You can play peekaboo with your baby for years: it is so enduring because it means different things at different stages of your baby's development.

Hide and reveal Your baby will wait with excitement as you play peekaboo. Hide your face behind a scarf, pull a hat over your eyes, or hide behind your hands then reveal your face with a flourish saying "Peekaboo."

I can see you Gently lay a light blanket, handkerchief or piece of lace across her face. Your baby or you could pull it away, then you can react with a surprised "There you are" as she is revealed. She'll enjoy the idea that you didn't know where she was.

It's still there Play games of hide and seek to reinforce the concept that objects exist even when they're out of your baby's sight. Hide teddy bears or blocks behind a cushion, under a cloth, or in a box and help him search until he finds them.

Pop-up puppets Play a game of appearing and disappearing with puppets or toys. Make them appear over the top of the sofa again and again, each time in a different place. She'll be on high alert as she watches for them.

Object permanence

Understanding that people and things still exist, even when they can't be seen, touched, or heard, is a landmark in your baby's cognitive development.

New understanding The concept of "object permanence" means that if your baby drops a toy and it's out of view, she will search for it because she knows it is there to be found. Object permanence begins to emerge as early as three months and is fully developed by around 12 months.

A separate person Before your baby figures out that objects are still there, she has grasped that you exist as a separate person even when she can't see or hear you. One way she shows this "person permanence" is by looking around for you when you are out of sight. This is also a step forward in the development of her own sense of self—her awareness that she is a separate individual, different from you or others.

10 to 12 months

YOUR BUSY BABY

Your baby is on the threshold of toddlerhood—
he is working hard to develop the skills needed to
walk, talk, and manage his world with greater ease.
Offering him plenty of praise and encouragement
will give him the confidence to try new things.

YOUR SOCIAL BABY

By the time he's one year old, your baby
will be starting to show an increased
interest in his wider social circle; although
he will still play on his own when in the
company of other children, he may watch
them from a distance and copy their play.

Your baby will start to become
increasingly independent and will want
to explore everywhere. However, he needs
to know that you're close by for him to feel
secure enough to leave your side. Despite
his new independence, he'll continue to
enjoy his established routines, which help
him feel secure. His emotional world is

developing, too. He is growing more aware
of his and others' feelings and emotions
and, by 12 months old, will start to become
more expressive, offering loving kisses
or pushing you away when he's feeling a
bit annoyed.

His self awareness is developing, and he's
beginning to understand how he and others
relate to each other, although he is not yet
overly aware of his own behavior.

GETTING MOVING

At around nine to 10 months, your baby will
probably have developed the ability to stay
upright while supported, and he may start

to side–step, or "cruise," around the room
while holding onto furniture. This is the
precursor to his first independent
steps—the milestone you've been waiting
for. Some babies are quicker to walk than
others. While a few manage to walk by 12
months, most tend to achieve this between
12 and 15 months. Be warned, though, that
the transition from his first tentative step
until he is fully walking can be a gradual
one, sometimes taking several weeks.

You can help your baby's mobility by
balancing the amount of time he spends
sitting still with opportunities for action,
since it will be during moments of play that
he makes his biggest developmental leaps,
and gains confidence. So try to make sure
he doesn't spend too long strapped into car
seats, high chairs, and strollers.

HAND CONTROL

It's around this time that your baby reaches
the significant milestone of being able to
control the small "pincer" movements of
his fingers, and by about 12–15 months he'll
refine this ability to hold objects between
his finger and thumb. This ability opens up
plenty of new learning opportunities for
your baby since he can now start managing
holding a spoon, brush, or chunky crayon.

In the following months, with plenty of
practice, your baby will become
increasingly accurate at directing his hands
to pick up objects large and small.

COMMUNICATION SKILLS

One of your baby's greatest achievements
in these early years will be his mastery of
speech. The more you communicate with
him through touching, looking, gesturing,
singing, and speaking, the better his
language development. By 10 months old,
he'll be putting two sounds together, for
example "ahgoo"; and by 12 months, he'll
have delighted you by calling you "mama"
or "dada," and will regularly use two to six
words that you can recognize.

His listening skills are also improving. He
is learning to wait for your responses, which

Gestures Your baby is really getting familar
now with new gestures and signs. Pointing
and reaching out are popular gestures
around this time and your baby will use
these more often to help get his message
or needs across to you.

Sizing up shapes Seeing, feeling, and
experimenting with shapes and sizes is
essential as your toddler learns how things
can be different or "fit" together. Posting
games and shape sorters help her
understand these concepts.

Stimulating activity Your increasingly active baby will love exciting new environments. A day out, such as a trip to the beach, will be a feast for his senses and will appeal to his new sense of adventure and exploration.

helps him understand the concept of taking turns. His comprehension is steadily improving, and by 12 months old, he'll respond to simple instructions or requests, such as "clap hands." Furthermore, his ever-growing confidence in using gestures and signals, such as waving "bye bye," means that he can really begin to make himself understood.

BRAIN POWER

Your baby is grasping concepts such as "in" and "out," which in turn enables him to understand the relevant positions of objects and people, and also helps to reinforce his understanding of object permanence (see p.105). He is also developing a sense of the different properties of objects, from textures to sizes, and, with your help, may start to draw comparisons. Imaginative play begins to emerge now and will continue to evolve, opening up a whole new world of play to your baby.

Fun with books As your baby's fingers and hands become more adept at managing toys and books, she'll rise to the challenge of a fun pull-flap book, her dexterity rewarded by the "surprise" she discovers under the flap.

Standing holding on At around 10 months old, your baby may start to pull herself up on furniture to a standing position. Help her practice standing by holding her hands to steady her. Soon she'll be "cruising" around the furniture.

Your social baby

Staying close by

Your increasingly confident baby wants to explore—as long as you're nearby. She no longer needs to be in your arms to feel secure: a glance at you or an occasional return to your side is enough to reassure her.

How these activities help your baby

Staying close to your baby so that she can see and hear you while she plays helps her:

★ **Feel safe and secure.** You are her safe base; your presence means your baby can concentrate on play knowing you will take care of her.

★ **Put some distance between you.** When you maintain a reassuring presence, your baby will be confident to move farther away to explore.

★ **Entertain herself.** Your baby needs play time on her own, as well as with you, so that she learns how to occupy herself, even if only briefly.

In her own world If your baby has toys next to her and knows you're near, she may play for up to 10 minutes on her own. Give her a few different toys, such as shape sorters, shakers, and a crinkly soft toy.

Checking in Even when playing happily, your baby needs to know you're keeping her in mind. Stop what you're doing every now and then to see how she's doing, and switch toys if necessary.

TOP TIP
If you're returning to work now, knowing that your baby now understands that you always return can make things easier. Reinforce this by saying a cheerful goodbye and telling her you'll be back later.

Close enough to see Your baby will entertain herself if you're within sight. Set her up in the same room on a mat with stacking blocks or toys, and she'll glance up regularly to check you're there, then play on.

A good viewpoint From his position in a high chair, your baby can see you easily while he plays. Twist and turn suction toys, wood peg puzzles or a small board book popped on his tray will hold his interest.

Your social baby

Expressing emotions

Show your emotions and your baby will show hers in return. The more demonstrative you are, the more comfortable she'll be expressing herself. Her early experience of affection sets her pattern for the future.

Act it out Your baby is learning about relationships as he plays. Play "pretend" and give his teddy bear a loving hug, or make up stories for his puppets to act out and show their feelings through their actions.

How these activities help your baby

When you show your emotions through actions, words, and stories you are helping your baby to:

★ **Hug and be hugged.** Accepting and giving affection sets a habit for how she relates to others, now and in the future.

★ **Express her feelings.** Your baby is experiencing a range of emotions and finding ways to show them through her behavior and body language.

★ **Gain awareness.** Your baby is learning about different emotions by watching you and noticing how you reflect back what she feels.

Cuddling and hugs The more you show physical affection to your baby, the more receptive she will be to displays of affection. Offer her a pat, stroke, big hug, or massage— don't wait for her to reach out for it herself.

Give love You are your baby's best role model. Whenever she sees you being affectionate toward other people, or even the family pet, she will copy you and grow secure in expressing her love this way too.

Your social baby

Snuggle up

Bedtime is your opportunity to cosy up with your baby. An established evening routine helps both of you to wind down and, more importantly, gives you the chance to enjoy each other's uninterrupted company. With a comforting bedtime routine, you and your baby can be at your closest.

How these activities help your baby

A good bedtime routine in a relaxed atmosphere helps your baby:

★ **Feel safe and secure.** Your reassuring presence and a calming routine helps your baby feel safe enough to surrender himself to sleep.

★ **Build your bond.** Quiet times when you can tune in to each other keep you and your baby feeling close.

In addition to...

★ **Get enough rest.** At this age, your baby needs about 14 hours sleep a day, including two daytime naps.

★ **Soothe himself.** Your baby's bedtime routine should signal him to relax in preparation for sleep.

Winding down When you follow the same bedtime pattern at the same time every night—for example, bathe and feed your baby, share a story, then tuck him up in his crib—he knows what to expect, and feels reassured.

TOP TIP
Bedtime routines established in your baby's first year not only benefit him here and now, but also set lasting positive sleep associations that will serve him well for many years.

Soothing touch Your baby may be relaxed by a light massage of his hands or feet, or gentle patting or stroking as he lies in his crib. Even a calm hand on his head or body reassures him that he's safe and can sleep.

Dim the lights Use low lighting and keep noise to a minimum in your baby's room. Blackout blinds can be useful in summer so your baby isn't disturbed by lighter nights. A warm, but not overheated, room helps too.

Story time There is something special about the quiet moments before bed when you and your baby can snuggle up and share a story or two. When you make this a regular part of his routine, you will help him set a reading habit for life.

Routines and your older baby

As your baby grows, an established routine will continue to be important. Although the activities will probably remain the same, you may want to adapt the routine slightly as he develops, for example, by extending story time.

Knowing what to expect Routines help your baby prepare for particular moments. A predictable chain of events acts as a signal for him about what is coming next and helps him to get ready. For example, when you get his clothes on and pop him in the stroller, he'll start to get excited since he anticipates a trip outdoors. Similarly, when you bathe him and snuggle up for a story, he will automatically begin to calm because this signals winding down for sleep time.

Being flexible during the day
Of course, it's not possible to have exactly the same routine every day, but if you can, try to keep the order in which you do things much the same. So the order of each day might be something like a wake-up routine, a morning and afternoon nap, playtime, visits or an outing, and then his usual bedtime routine. This framework allows you to structure the day, although the exact timing of events may be different as you respond to his needs when he's sleepy, hungry, or ready to play a little earlier or later.

Your social baby

In good company

Your baby has a lot of friends to make, and she's ready to meet them. You will be her social planner, taking her to parent and baby groups, baby activities, and family gatherings. She'll show her interest in other babies by looking and touching, but will only play if you are involved.

How these activities help your baby

When you give your baby the opportunity to be around other babies and children you are helping her:

★ **Be comfortable with her peers.** Simply being around other babies is the first step to being social.

★ **Look and learn.** Your baby will stake out her future playmates by watching them first, before she moves on, in future months, to playing close by them.

★ **Explore.** She's finding out about other babies, what they feel and look like and how they react.

★ **Practice with brothers and sisters.** Play and interaction led by and kept going by her siblings means that your baby has the opportunity to practice being social with a familiar partner.

Happy to look Your baby likes to play with you or by herself, but she's not yet ready to join other children or on her own. Give her opportunities to watch children, and talk to her about what they're doing: observing is the start of her social contact.

TOP TIP

Don't underestimate the value of friendships forged in playgroups. The friends your baby makes now may stay with her through the preschool, and even into the school years.

Are you real? At this stage your baby is an eager explorer and may approach other children as objects to be discovered. Encourage older children to be patient as she touches, looks at, and tries to move them.

What are you like? Your baby is learning about her peers by really staring at them. Let her watch other babies from your lap, seated near them at playgroups, or during activities such as baby yoga.

Regular playmate It is easier for your baby to be social with a familiar brother or sister than her peer group. Supervize as your older and youngest children play peekaboo, roll a ball back and forth, or converse in words and babbles.

Self awareness

I'm me! Your baby is starting to understand that she is separate from you. The first signs of this come before she's three months old when she turns to find you after you have moved out of sight.

Understanding the world Your baby has a sense now of "person permanence": the realization that you exist even when she can't see or hear you. Her self awareness builds as she discovers her own body and her increasing control over it. She's also developing a mental picture of herself and the people she knows. By around 12 months, she can differentiate between a photograph of herself and that of another baby. Later, at around 15 months comes the revelation that the image in a mirror is herself.

Acting out Another sign that your baby is aware of herself and others is her fantasy play. When she acts out cuddling her teddy, bear or offers it a pretend drink, she's copying others' behavior.

Growing awareness At this stage, your baby's self awareness isn't acute. It won't be until she's into her second year that she really starts to assert herself and become conscious of her behavior, for example, by showing embarrassment or by looking ashamed.

Mom and me Becoming more aware of her independent status is a significant milestone for your baby, and she may check regularly that you're still there.

Getting moving

Cruise control

Your baby's mobility takes a leap forward as he stays upright and "cruises" the furniture, holding on and side–stepping until he can go no further. Be prepared for his first tentative step!

How these activities help your baby

When you encourage your baby to cruise the furniture and stand alone you are helping him:

★ **Achieve balance.** Side–stepping helps your baby's stability and coordination, preparing him for walking.

★ **Get stronger.** All this movement is good exercise for his leg muscles.

★ **Practice stepping.** He's lifting his feet and planting them as he cruises, and may also practice stepping movements as he stands.

★ **Get what he wants.** Your baby is striving for more independence—improved mobility means he's able to get more things for himself.

Side–stepping Your baby will love to cruise when you place toys for him to work toward. Put a toy or teddy bear a few feet from him on the sofa so he must side–step to reach it.

Stand alone Once she's a competent cruiser, try placing chairs a little apart so she has to bridge a gap to move from one to the other and, briefly, stand unaided.

Come into my arms When you reach out to your baby, he may be willing to let go of the furniture and step into your arms if you are very close, or side–step across a small gap between chair and sofa to get his hug.

KEY FACT
If your baby was premature, he'll probably reach milestones a little later. Avoid anxiety by measuring his development based on his due date rather than his birth date.

Getting moving

Dropping and throwing

Away it goes: your baby has discovered the fun in dropping and throwing his toys and balls. He'll experiment with how many times you are prepared to bring back the toy he drops, and will try large and small movements as he practices releasing his grip to let things fly.

How these activities help your baby

As your baby drops or throws his toys and balls and you join in, you are helping him:

★ Fine tune his movements. Your baby is learning when to release his grip as he moves to throw a ball.

★ Practice hand–eye coordination. Throwing improves your baby's ability to aim as well as his muscle control.

★ Be active. He'll be crawling and side–stepping around the room as he chases the balls he's scattered.

You are also helping him:

★ Have fun. Rolling, throwing, and dropping balls—there's so much entertainment to be had from such a simple object.

Drop and pick up This is a favorite game for your baby. She'll drop her toy out of her stroller or high chair so you can pick it up and give it back, then she'll repeat the sequence again—and again and again.

Soft and squishy Whether he's dropping, patting, or throwing, he'll find it easier with a bean bag or squashy ball. Guide him through basic throwing: gently raise his hand, palm out, and then pivot at the elbow.

Throw and scoop Give your baby a variety of items to throw—try scrunched up paper for a lightweight and easy-to-clasp option for her to toss around. A baby ball pit allows her to churn or scoop the balls up with swoops of her arms.

TOP TIP

In addition to being fun, dropping and throwing help your baby to estimate short-range distances, which in turn helps his passing skills.

Hand control

Splashing around

Splashing, pouring, and squeezing: there's so much to do with water and it's such good practice for your baby's fine movements and muscle control. Water play is ideal for practicing skills—the spills are all part of the fun.

How these activities help your baby

When you introduce water play in a bowl, bath, or paddling pool with different toys and containers to handle, you are helping your baby:

★ Grasp and manipulate different shapes and weights. Your baby is working hard on balancing things in her hand, turning and tipping objects of different sizes.

★ Rehearse fine movements. An added benefit of water play is that your baby gets to practice the small muscle control of her wrist, hands, and fingers.

★ Strengthen her grip. Squeezing and squirting help to exercise the muscles used to grasp.

In addition to...

★ Reinforce cause and effect. Tipping, pouring, and squeezing all give the satisfaction of a clear result for your baby's actions.

KEY FACT

For safety's sake, never leave your baby unsupervised in or near water, no matter how shallow, even for a moment.

Squeeze, squeak, squirt Sponges, squirters, and squeaky toys let your baby practice gripping and squeezing. Give her sponges of different sizes to soak then squeeze, help her fill then squirt from a toy, or watch her delight as she "squeaks" her duck.

Grip and tip Your baby will have fun and fine tune the small movements of her hand and wrist as she fills plastic cups, small pitchers, or a mini watering can with water and empties them with a splash in the bath.

Float and fill Use a big bowl for short bursts of water play. Let her choose plastic animals to float and catch. Fill a colander then watch as the water leaks away, or take turns filling and tipping pitchers.

Cause and effect Water play combines the coordination to hold and pour with a nice splashy result. Your baby will enjoy the outcome when he pours water into a toy that sends wheels spinning as it pours through, or fills up a bucket until it sinks.

Communication skills

Taking turns

Your baby is learning that there is more to speaking than simply making sounds. He needs to wait and listen as well as express himself. With practice, he'll enjoy the give and take that games and conversation offer.

How these activities help your baby

By playing turn-taking games, asking and answering questions, and holding conversations, you're helping your baby:

★ **Wait his turn.** Communication is based on giving and receiving messages: games and conversation develop this skill.

★ **Engage you in conversation.** Your baby is playing a greater part in keeping a "conversation" going by listening and then responding.

★ **Realize he is understood.** Your baby is learning that his sounds and gestures have meaning for you.

In addition to...

★ **Tolerate waiting.** Turn taking helps him deal with short periods of waiting.

Listen and reply As your baby puts together sounds such as "ah goo" or "ma ma" repeat them, wait for his reaction, then reply. Keep up this back and forth conversation.

My turn, your turn Practice turn taking by passing toys back and forth to your baby saying "Here it is" each time. Sit on the floor opposite each other and roll a ball to him, then encourage him to roll it back to you as you say "Your turn."

Communication skills

Describe and compare

The more detail you give, the greater your baby's command of language. Enrich his understanding by describing and making comparisons. He won't name colors or textures for a while, but he's starting to comprehend.

So many colors Your baby is ready to hear about colors now. As he touches a block or toy say "That's green" or "The block is red." Start with primary colors, because these are easier for him to distinguish than more subtle shades.

How these activities help your baby

When your chatter is filled with clear descriptions and comparisons you are helping your baby:

★ Improve his vocabulary. The greater variety of words your baby hears, the larger his vocabulary will be in the months to come.

★ Label the properties of objects. Your baby is learning to put names to colors, size, and textures.

★ Make comparisons. Your baby is just getting to know that objects can be grouped according to their size, color, and other categories.

Compare and contrast Your baby is starting to understand concepts such as bigger and smaller. Help her by using these labels in everyday chat. Say "Here is your small teddy bear" when you show it to her, or offer two toys and ask "Show me the big one."

Soft and hard Introduce your baby to words that tell him about texture by labeling them as he touches things. When he cuddles a fluffy toy ask him "Is it soft?" If he nods, you get the chance to agree and say "Yes, it's soft" to reinforce the word.

Communication skills

Understanding meaning

Your baby is putting words and meaning together to figure out what you're saying. Her comprehension is more advanced than her ability to talk: she understands simple sentences, although she says only one or two words.

How these activities help your baby

When you keep your baby busy with questions and clear instructions you are helping her:

★ **Understand simple requests.** Ask her just one thing at a time and your baby will be able to figure out what you want.

★ **Act on what you ask.** When you make a request, then point and nod encouragement, you are helping your baby understand what to do.

★ **Cooperate.** Your delight when your baby follows an instruction tells her that this earns your approval.

Following requests Your baby wants to please you and will enjoy bringing over something you've requested. Ask him something simple like "Bring me the book" or "Get the cup" and point to the object to help him understand what you mean.

Give me a kiss Your baby can understand and obey some simple instructions. Make sure you only ask her to do one thing at a time, for example "Give me a kiss" or "Please drink your milk"—she's not ready for anything more complicated.

KEY FACT
By 10 months, your baby is becoming attuned to intonation and will still understand a word if it's said with a different emphasis or by a less familiar person.

Little helper Your baby will really get the hang of doing what you ask when you share jobs together. Give her clear instructions like "Put the toy in the basket" and put one in yourself to demonstrate. Then she can follow both your request and your example.

(Brain power)

In and out

Your baby is learning about the positions of people and objects. They can be in or out, behind, or over and under. This helps him make sense of what happens when he sorts, pushes, balances, or covers up his toys.

How these activities help your baby

By playing with games, books and toys that involve putting things in, out, under and over you are helping your baby:

★ Build up his understanding of position. Your baby is creating a mental model of the world, including how objects relate to each other.

★ Put a name to the concepts he's grasping. These verbal labels create a shorthand for the ideas that your baby is learning.

★ Get to know the rules of how objects behave. Through play, your baby is finding out how objects balance, fall over, and move.

★ Build his understanding of object permanence. Sorting-box toys and hide-and-seek games are good activities to show your baby that things still exist when he can't see or hear them.

Disappearing shapes Your baby learns the concepts of "in" and "out" through play. He'll start to enjoy shape sorters now; he'll love to watch things disappear, then be revealed as he takes them out.

Empty and full As your baby empties and fills his toy box, or pours water out of a bath container, remind him of the concepts he's learning by naming them, saying "The cup is empty" or "The box is full."

Under and over Let your baby experience different positions as he plays. Crawl around together under the table (supervising closely so he doesn't bang his head) or behind the sofa, describing each position to him.

Read about it Build up anticipation as you wonder with your baby what could be under or behind the flap as a story unfolds. Choose books that include the ideas of under, over, in, and out so that they become familiar.

KEY FACT
By 10 months, your baby's improved dexterity and understanding lead him to explore more with his hands than with his mouth; by 12 months, he seldom "mouths" objects.

Drop it Whether you help your baby put your letters in the mailbox, push a doorbell, or put pegs in a bag, he'll be happy to be your helper. These real life tasks are another opportunity to learn about position.

Young explorer Your mobile baby is experiencing different positions for himself as he climbs into and out of a box to play house, goes under the table, through a tunnel, or over the edge of his play gym.

Age-appropriate toys

Playtime should be fun first and foremost, but you will also want your baby to be stimulated and to learn from the toys you offer.

Choosing toys Look for toys that match your baby's age—most items state the appropriate age range on the packaging. In addition, take your child's developmental stage into account. Every baby develops at a different rate, so choose toys to suit his individual mobility, dexterity, and understanding.

Presenting a challenge Give your baby toys that challenge or stretch him. If a toy is too easy, he will be bored quickly. However, one that's too hard for him to use can result in frustration. To get maximum play and learning value, your baby should have to use some thought or effort to make the activity or toy work.

Toys to grow with Choose toys that can be used at several levels of complexity. Play foods, for example, can be ideal for your younger baby to tip and sort, but can also be used as he matures for playing shopping or other imaginary play.

Try it out Try before you buy. Find out what engages your baby by borrowing toys from friends or family before purchasing one.

Brain power

Exploring texture

It's a feast for her senses as your baby touches, strokes, and sees the different textures and surfaces around her. Encourage her to explore soft, hard, rough, and smooth textures, and name each one to help her label them and categorize all the information she is receiving.

How these activities help your baby

When you point out textures and encourage your baby to explore objects through touch, you are helping her:

★ **Feed her senses and her brain.** Your baby is storing information from all of her senses to understand what she sees and feels.

★ **Create categories.** Your baby's brain is primed to organize and group information. In the coming months, she will figure out that her stuffed animals can be classified as "things that are soft" and her blocks categorized as hard.

★ **Understand "same" and "different."** Looking at and feeling different textures shows your baby how to make comparisons and find similarities.

★ **Improve her vocabulary.** Use lots of descriptions to add to her word list.

Softly, softly Guide your baby's hand as she strokes the soft fur of her toy animals or holds a woolly scarf up to her cheek. Fluffiness is a texture she will find pleasing and even comforting.

Compare textures Different surfaces feel as well as look different. Give your baby a chance to look at and touch a variety of textured toys, blocks, and balls, and describe each one to her as she does.

KEY FACT

Touching is integral to your baby's understanding of the world. By now, even if she can't see an object, touching it helps her create a mental image that helps her identify it.

Hard edges Blocks, bricks, and sturdy plastic toys all give your baby clear edges and solidity to feel. She's learning about these properties as she weighs objects in her hands and explores them through touch.

Fluffy, smooth, and rough Some interactive baby books introduce textures as well as the descriptive words that go with them. Find books that invite your baby to touch textured patches as the story progresses: she might feel the scales of a crocodile, the furry tummy of a chick, or the shiny smoothness of a mirror.

Your baby's developing brain

Your baby's brain, her higher brain or cortex particularly, is now developing faster than at any other time in her life.

Making connections It's feedback from your baby's senses that creates and enriches the pathways in her brain. Everything she sees, hears, tastes, smells, and touches helps her form connections and build mental maps of her environment.

Learning through repetition Your baby will quickly learn things that are repeated frequently. This is because repetition strengthens the connections between her brain cells. Conversely, pathways that are rarely used fall away and connections are lost: this is the brain's way of ensuring that the strongest, most effective pathways dominate.

New concepts At around 12 months old, the mental maps and collected information in your baby's brain allow her to grasp some big ideas. Object permanence is well established (see p.105) and she has started to understand cause and effect, object relationships, such as "in," "on," and "under," and to use her imagination.

Development throughout infancy By the time your baby reaches five years old, 90 percent of her brain development has been completed. All this activity doesn't increase the number of brain cells, of which there are over 100 billion, but does form the connections between cells through which information is passed and learning occurs.

1 year to 18 months

YOUR NEW TODDLER

In the course of a year, your baby has developed from an alert newborn into an active, curious toddler. From walking and talking to increased manual dexterity, your toddler's accelerating skills mean that his world is rapidly expanding.

YOUR SOCIAL BABY

Over the following year, your baby's social world will change subtly as he gradually moves away from solitary play and begins to play happily closely alongside other children, known as "parallel" play. Other than the lack of direct interaction that characterizes this stage of play, the concept of sharing is also still unfamiliar to your baby. He is very much the center of his world and doesn't understand the need to share with others, which means that play between toddlers requires close supervision. Turn taking is a fairly new concept too. Although he may be learning the art of taking turns when he communicates and listens, he is not ready to apply this to his play with other children.

Your baby's awareness of your feelings continues to grow, and by 18 months, you may notice him watching you to see if you approve of his actions, and expressing his own feelings more clearly. He's also starting to imitate you more, and will be eager to join you in some practical tasks. This will be matched by a drive for independence as he makes it clear that he wants to try certain things himself, such as opening a door, or feeding himself. Letting him have a try is important for his confidence and learning.

GETTING MOVING

At around 12 to 15 months, your baby will probably be taking his first steps. As with crawling, walking, climbing, and running all require different parts of his body to work together for movement to happen. Once he does start to walk and his balance improves, the playground will open up to him and he'll start to tackle toddler slides and other basic playground equipment.

Not every baby develops as quickly as the next and, while most infants gain skills in roughly the same order, a few may miss one step, for example, bottom shuffling instead of crawling. It can be tempting to compare how your baby moves with the progress of others his age. This may be helpful if you're concerned that your child is delayed. However, there is plenty of variation in normal physical development, so don't worry if he is not at quite the same stage as his playmate. Unless he's showing no signs of walking by 18 months old, there's unlikely to be any cause for concern.

Stacking up Wooden blocks, or shapes that can be stacked or built, exercise several of your toddler's abilities. Successfully putting things together involves both thinking, balance, and manual dexterity.

Make my mark As your toddler's ability to hold and manipulate objects improves, she'll enjoy using a paintbrush or chunky crayon. Give her plenty of paper and bright colors to get her going.

Standing up At last, your toddler is on his own two feet and taking his first shaky steps. In addition to managing to propel himself forward, he's also learning to balance and will hone this skill over the coming months.

HAND CONTROL

Your toddler is continuing to consolidate his manual skills. As his hand–eye coordination steadily improves, he will not only be able to play with more intricate toys, but will also begin to master the art of holding a chunky crayon or paintbrush. As a result, he may start to indulge in plenty of scribbling. This is the perfect time to introduce him to creative pursuits and messy play with paints, playdough, crayon, and chalk.

You may start to wonder whether your toddler is left- or right-handed, and by 18 months, you should notice a preference.

COMMUNICATION SKILLS

Your toddler will be adding new words to his vocabulary at a rapid pace now: he may say as many as 20 words by 18 months old and will understand the meaning of many more. He may also begin to put two words together to make his first simple sentences.

His assertiveness grows steadily, and you might well find that his favorite word is "no," which he may use consistently! At 18 months, he's reading your expression and, if you cry or laugh, he may do it too.

BRAIN POWER

As your toddler's understanding of different concepts, such as cause and effect, grows, he starts to show an interest in how things work—for example, how different parts of a train track fit together or how blocks build up. His imaginative play is growing and he begins to take an interest in role play. In addition, his memory is steadily improving and he will start to store more information in his long-term memory. For example, he will be able to find items and toys always kept in the same place and will be comfortable with the layout of his home and other very familiar environments.

New experiences As your toddler's curiosity about her world grows, she'll love to be introduced to new sights and sounds. Strumming on a guitar will fascinate her and she'll love the effect her actions make.

Side by side Your toddler's social world is slowly opening up and he will begin to enjoy playing alongside regular "playmates"; although there's little contact, each will be happily engaged in his own separate activity.

Your social baby

The art of copying

You are your toddler's most important role model: he'll want to imitate what you do and say. He's driven to copy by a desire to be like you. He's primed to learn and all the time he's noticing and practicing how you relate to other people, do everyday chores, and enjoy yourself.

How these activities help your toddler

When you give your baby opportunities to copy you and act out familiar scenes, you are helping him:

★ Notice how people treat each other. He's learning about relationships by watching how you relate to others.

★ Try out his social skills. Social situations can be complicated. Imaginative play helps your toddler practice roles and social behaviors.

★ Feel close to you. Mirroring your behavior allows your toddler to maintain his bond with you.

★ Practice new behaviors. Watching then copying is a good way for your toddler to learn.

Let me help Your toddler wants to join in with what the grown-ups do. He'll enjoy the social atmosphere in the kitchen. Give him a bowl of cake mix to stir before you bake or let him help mash some potatoes.

Take a picture Your toddler will feel proud when he takes photos just like you. Guide his hands onto the buttons, then pose as he clicks. Look at and talk about the photos afterward to add to the experience.

Role play Give your toddler toys that help her mimic your actions. She can practice social skills as she holds her toy phone and "talks," or do practical tasks as she puts a teddy bear in the stroller or stirs a spoon.

Green fingers There's plenty of potential for companionship when you work together outside. Get his bucket and spade so he can dig next to you, or enlist his help to water the plants, or rub a sponge on the car.

KEY FACT
The early years are crucial ones in terms of learning. During this time, your child is thought to learn more than at any other time during his life.

Make housework fun Turn daily chores into playtime by putting on some music or nursery rhymes and sing as you clean up. Your toddler can join in by using his own duster or broom just like yours, or you can share jobs.

Being a good role model

Your toddler watches your every move and copies your behavior, language, and how you relate to other people. Being his role model is a big responsibility, but it's also a good opportunity to pass on the best of yourself to him.

Social skills When you're warm and respectful to others, your toddler will copy this behavior. If you regularly say "please" and "thank you," he's more likely to use good manners, too, as his social skills grow.

Gender differences Your toddler can tell the difference between men and women and is a sharp observer of the behavior of both. How you act, and your role within the home, will influence how he views the responsibilities of men and women.

Language Your toddler is a sponge for new words and will pick up on terms or sayings you use frequently. Whatever you say, consider how it will sound coming from his mouth in the months to come.

Interests and hobbies As a family, the interest you show in outdoor activities, sports, movies, theater, or culture, all help shape your toddler's preferences in the future.

Your social baby

Playing side by side

Your toddler is fascinated by other children but is still not ready to join in. Keep playtime peaceful by setting up parallel play—sit friends together with their own blocks, paints, or playdough and they'll happily play alongside each other. You'll need to supervise, though, since sharing may be an issue.

How these activities help your toddler

By taking her to play groups and encouraging your toddler to play alongside others you are helping her:

★ Get used to being with others her own age. Gradually build up her circle of toddler friends so she feels comfortable in small, then larger, groups.

★ Improve her social skills. Every social contact allows her to practice looking, smiling, and vocalizing at her peers.

★ Begin to play with others. Playing side-by-side is the starting point for your toddler in the world of social play.

Aware of others As your toddler gets used to playing near others, he may copy the actions of a child nearby—this is a step toward engaging each other in play. Notice as he watches then imitates simple actions, such as digging or pouring in the sand.

Joining in Organized activities, where your toddler joins with others to sing a song or do action rhymes, help her recognize she is part of a group. Take her to toddler groups and playgrounds so she gets used to busier, noisier, situations. Join in yourself and she will be more comfortable taking part.

Learning to share

Your toddler quite naturally sees herself as the center of the universe, and it will be a while before she grasps the concept of sharing.

Your toddler's world She considers everything belongs to her, and her needs rule the daily lives of those around her. This is a normal egocentric stage of development, and your toddler finds it almost impossible to see things from anyone else's point of view. Being aware of this particular stage can be useful in understanding her behavior. For example, it makes sense that she is angry and upset when another child takes a toy off her because she sees this object as belonging to her. For an adult, this would be the equivalent of someone walking over and taking your handbag, wallet, or driving off with your car. So supervise closely and be ready to intervene if you see your toddler about to grab toys off other children, and step in before others snatch in return.

Helping her share You can help your toddler develop the social skill of sharing by praising her if she offers a toy or food to you or another child. Expect this to be a gradual learning process, not completed until she's around five years old!

Parallel play Your toddler is ready to play alongside another child, but not to get involved with them. Set up activities such as train, car, farm, or zoo sets so your toddler and a playmate have enough equipment to play side by side. Remember to supervise closely to avoid conflict over toys.

Your social baby

Growing independence

The drive to be independent begins around this age. Your determined toddler will shrug off your help with dressing or eating. Guide him through these self-help tasks and give him time to try out new skills. Know when to step in and when to give him room to keep trying.

How these activities help your baby

By giving your toddler time and encouragement to try dressing or feeding himself you are helping him:

★ **Try it out.** He's striving to do more for himself and needs a lot of practice to properly master complicated tasks, such as using a spoon.

★ **Take it a step at a time.** Break down complicated tasks into small steps that he can achieve.

★ **Gain confidence and satisfaction.** He's building up a sense of self-efficacy —that he can do things for himself.

In addition to...

★ **See that you believe in him.** As you show that you have confidence in him, he will gain self-confidence too.

Eating together Create social mealtimes by sitting down with your toddler to eat. You are teaching him table manners, showing him how to use cutlery, and creating a habit of sharing conversation as well as food.

TOP TIP

Although trying out things herself helps your toddler learn skills, boundaries are still important. Supervision is essential, and if something isn't safe, he needs to know it's not okay.

I can feed myself It's messy, but worth it, as your toddler tries to feed herself. Sit with her and use a spoon too so she can copy. Guide her hands to keep the spoon level, but don't take over—she wants to do it herself.

Practice makes perfect Like most new skills, your toddler will practice them in his imaginative play. As he holds a spoon to his stuffed animal's mouth or puts a cup to his lips he is refining his ability as well as role-playing mealtimes.

Letting your child try it

"Me do it" is your toddler's way of saying he is ready to be more independent. He's experiencing a desire to practice new skills until he has mastered them. This enthusiasm to try out new things will be an advantage throughout life.

Being patient On an everyday basis, there will be delays while your toddler tries to feed himself or put on his coat. This can be frustrating and you may be tempted to take over, but try to resist, since this will only make matters worse and you'll have to battle him for control.

Making time Try some practical remedies, such as leaving more time for each activity, or getting up earlier to start the morning routine. As he gets better at each task, he'll be quicker to complete it and there will be less delay.

Help him out Actively teach him some key self-help skills, such as getting his clothes on. Set up practice sessions when there is no time pressure, such as weekend mornings or getting dressed after swimming. Break down tasks into small steps and go through each one, perhaps telling him what to do and guiding him physically if he needs any help with a task.

Last but not least Show your toddler how to dress by putting her clothes on part way and letting her do the last little bit. For example, she could pull down her T-shirt once it's over her head and arms. When she accomplishes each small step, let her do more the next time.

(Getting moving)

Totter and tumble

Your coordinated toddler is ready to walk. She'll start with a wide legged, bandy step, which gives her most stability. Practice makes perfect, so get her out of the stroller and onto her feet every chance you get.

How these activities help your toddler

When you encorage your toddler to take steps outdoors and in—even just a few at a time—you are helping her:

★ **Start walking.** Your toddler is making the transition from pulling up and side-stepping to stepping forward. By 13 months, about half of toddlers can walk.

★ **Keep her balance.** It's through practice that your toddler's balance and coordination improve.

★ **Get around.** Her growing mobility means that your toddler can make more choices about what to do and where she wants to explore.

Stepping around Clear some space so that she can take steps without too much in the way. Set the furniture a little farther apart, or so he can walk around it, to encourage him to walk without hanging on for balance as he gets around.

TOP TIP

If your toddler is not walking by 18 months, it's recommended that you seek advice and reassurance from a pediatrician.

Step by step Build his confidence by standing behind him and holding his hands, or in front of him, holding his hands as he steps toward you. Walk at his pace, keeping your arms relaxed so you're not pulling.

Sure footed As your toddler becomes a more confident walker, she'll challenge her balance and coordination by managing pull- or push-a-long toys as she walks, starting to carry things and speeding up her steps.

Finding a balance

It's all a matter of balance for your newly walking toddler. She's upright and wants to twist, turn, and bend her body without landing with a bump. Stimulate her balance with activities that keep her body in motion.

Bend down, straighten up Your toddler practices complicated movements and balance through her play. On family outings, she'll bend, reach, and turn to collect leaves and feathers on a nature trail or look for shells and pebbles on the beach.

How these activities help your toddler

Activities that involve reaching, balancing and stretching help your toddler:

★ Bend, twist, and turn. Now that she's walking, your toddler has new postures and movements to learn, such as staying on her feet while she moves at the waist.

★ Enjoy her moving body. Your toddler's increasingly smooth and stable control of her body means that she can move with confidence.

★ Move her weight from one foot to another. To step and then run, your toddler needs to gain confidence moving her weight from one foot to the other.

Stomp and splash Now she's upright, every time your toddler stamps and splashes in a muddy puddle or paddling pool, she'll be balancing on one foot and coordinating the other—great for her balance and good practice for walking.

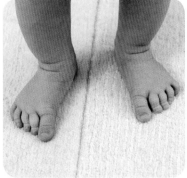

Feedback from her feet When she goes barefoot, your toddler is using her toes to grip and flex for a steadier walk, and her skin sends information about her posture to her brain. Keep her shoeless as much as you can indoors and on safe, even surfaces outside.

Getting moving

Gaining stability

Your toddler is learning to climb, ride, and swing. Her ability to correct herself and keep herself from falling comes with practice. You'll spend lots of time supervising her as she becomes more stable.

How these activities help your toddler

When you give your toddler regular opportunities to ride, climb, float, and bounce, you are helping her:

★ **Find her balance.** The parts of your toddler's brain responsible for balance use feedback from each movement she makes to improve her stability.

★ **Coordinate her movements.** Your toddler is holding her body at different angles and working her arms and legs together to correct her balance.

★ **Gain confidence.** It can be unsettling to be off-balance. The more your toddler is introduced to different movements, the more willing she'll be to keep trying.

Scoot along Ride-on toys and tricycles are ideal to give your toddler stability while he balances and moves himself forward and back, stops and starts. He's coordinating his arms, legs, and feet and staying upright.

Different dimensions The greater variety of movement your toddler experiences, the more she gains balance. At the playground let her climb, slide, go on the swings, try the seesaw, and bounce on a toddler trampoline.

TOP TIP
Let your toddler go at her own pace in the pool and put the emphasis on fun. If she's reluctant to go under, don't try to persuade her, or she may develop a dislike of water play that takes a while to undo.

Float and move The buoyancy created by water allows your toddler to experience different movements. Pull her through the water in her swim ring, bob her up and down and twirl her in a circle to give her different sensations.

Getting moving

Up and down stairs

Those stairs look like a mountain to your toddler, but she wants to try them and has enough coordination and balance to do it. Help her experiment with different methods from bottom shuffling to careful steps.

Bottom shuffle Bumping down each step on his bottom, using his arms push-up style behind him, is one way to get down the stairs, especially when encouraged by a sibling. Stay close by though, because he may topple while he's learning.

How these activities help your toddler

As you gain confidence in her ability to balance and encourage her to practice moving up and down the stairs, you are helping your toddler:

★ Master climbing steps. Being able to manage stairs is a key mobility skill for your independent toddler.

★ Improve her coordination. To step up and down smoothly, your toddler must use her skills of balance and synchronization of movement.

★ Gain confidence. To your toddler, it can seem a long way from the top of the stairs to the bottom. Each time she achieves it shows her she has enough control to keep herself from falling.

Forward facing Going up and down stairs on her tummy, or holding the bannister, facing the steps, may feel like the safest method for your toddler. Stay close and make sure each step is clear of obstacles.

Step up With a steadying hand from you, your toddler can walk up or down steps putting both feet onto each step as she goes. As she gains confidence, she may start to do this hanging onto the stair rail.

TOP TIP

Toddler gym play sessions with soft blocks to climb on and cushioned mats to fall onto are great for your toddler to practice the skills needed to climb and balance.

Getting moving

Challenging activities

Your energetic toddler is ready to be more adventurous. He's enjoying exploring his surroundings and getting around. Put his new mobility to the test with physical activities and challenges that give him the chance to try out new movements and discover what he can do.

How these activities help your toddler

When you give your toddler plenty of opportunities for active, challenging play in different settings you are helping him:

★ Stretch himself. When he's having fun, he'll attempt new moves and angles without actually realizing he's trying something different.

★ Build his stamina. The more active he is, the stronger his muscles and staying power will become.

★ Educate his brain on how his body moves and coordinates. Your toddler is growing, and so the mental image of his body must change too. Feedback from his senses keeps his brain up to date.

Obstacle course Let your toddler test his skills in a playground obstacle course. Help him to climb through a low tire, or hold his hand while he stands on balancing logs or wobbly bridges.

KEY FACT

Getting your toddler into the habit of doing physical activity early reduces the chance of childhood obesity later and starts him off on a healthy footing.

Dance to the music Holding hands or clapping together, your toddler will find himself swaying and moving to music. Use nursery rhyme CDs, sing yourself, or play your own favorite songs to get him dancing.

Wiggle around Put out a toddler tunnel, or pretend to be wiggly worms sliding across the floor. Moving on hands and knees and wiggling on his tummy or back give your toddler different perspectives as he moves.

Climb and scramble Make use of equipment at the park or at home for a variety of balancing games. Stay close by (or if necessary hold his hand) as he navigates a toddler playground, or play a simple version of hide-and-seek in the back yard.

Assessing the risks

As your toddler grows more adventurous, you may be constantly tempted to step in. It's important, though, for him to try new activities, so you'll need to learn when to intervene and when to stand back and let him continue.

Trial and error It's through constant practice that your toddler's walking, climbing, and coordination advance. This means he is taking a bit of a risk as he's not entirely sure he can balance, step, or climb—but stumbles and bumps are all part of the learning experience.

When to step in It's important for your toddler's development that his play puts him a little off balance sometimes so that he learns how to correct his position by moving his arms and legs. The delicate balance between giving him the chance to test his developing mobility and keeping him safe may cause you some anxiety as he wobbles, trips, or falls. There will be times when you feel some moves or equipment are too dangerous to try on his own. Guide him by holding his hands or waist, or stay close enough to reach him before he falls.

Keeping watch No matter what he is doing, constant supervision is needed to keep your toddler safe and entertained. It's safe to assume that he will now explore all over your home and yard, so check those places you thought he couldn't reach to make sure he can't hurt himself.

Getting moving

Music and movement

Rhythm comes naturally to your toddler and he will be marvelously unselfconscious as he moves to music. Share his pleasure as he coordinates his moves to the tempo of a rhyme or song. Introduce him to your favorite songs, and dance together for fun and to feel close.

How these activities help your toddler

When you sing, dance, and play musical games together you are helping your toddler:

★ **Develop his coordination and increase muscle strength.** Turning and twirling challenges him to balance as he moves, and the activity strengthens his muscles and joints.

★ **Get into active habits.** Dancing is an excellent way to keep your toddler moving around.

★ **Build confidence.** There is no correct way for your toddler to dance—encourage him to try any move he wants and praise him on his dancing.

In addition to...

★ **Enhance his communication.** As your toddler listens and dances to different songs, he learns about sequences, words, and rhymes.

★ **Feel close to you.** The movements, touch and shared rhythms of dance and song strengthen your bond.

Sit and sway Movement to music doesn't always have to be big and bouncy. You and your toddler can enjoy gentler, smaller moves to soothing lullabies and soft, slow songs. Wave your hands and sway or rock her in your arms as you sing or listen to music.

Dance together As you dance with your toddler, match your movements to the tempo of the music: quick steps or twirls to a fast beat or gentle swaying when it's slow.

Natural rhythm Your toddler will move to music without thinking about it. Encourage her to dance any way she wants, then join in, matching her moves like her mirror image.

Musical games Your toddler will want to play over and over as he masters the actions to musical rhymes. Try the Hokey Pokey, "Head, shoulders, knees, and toes," and "The wheels on the bus" while you hold or guide his hands for balance.

Hand control

Bon appetit!

Your determined toddler wants to feed herself and she's got the grip to do it. The precision of her finger and hand movements and increasing hand–eye coordination mean she's ready to try out easy-grip cutlery and cups. Watch out for the mess—her food may not make it to her mouth.

How these activities help your toddler

By giving her every opportunity to feed herself with a spoon, try different foods, and use a cup you are helping her:

★ **Refine her grip.** The different texture and consistency of food means your toddler must keep adjusting her grasp.

★ **Increase her accuracy.** The more she repeats the moves that take food and drink to her mouth, the better your toddler's precision.

★ **Promote her independence.** She's determined to help herself and gets great satisfaction in the process.

KEY FACT
By now, not only has your toddler's grip improved, but she also has greater flexibility in her wrist, which allows her to rotate and aim her spoon with more accuracy.

Spoon to mouth Your toddler is learning to dig his spoon into his food, and tries to keep the spoon level long enough to get it into his mouth. Easy-grip spoons and food that's not too sloppy will make it easier for him.

Don't mind the mess Whether your toddler is missing her mouth with her spoon or squeezing, tipping, and squashing her food, she will make a mess at mealtimes. Try not to be too concerned about keeping her clean—it's a natural side effect of feeding herself.

Finger foods Picnics, either outdoors or on a rug in the living room, are ideal for introducing lots of different finger foods and trying a two-handled cup. As his grip grows more precise, he'll feed himself with ever greater accuracy.

Family mealtimes

Eating together is good for you and your toddler. There is plenty of evidence that when families eat together, children have a healthier, more balanced diet, gain a sense of belonging through talk, and learn new and different words since conversation covers plenty of topics.

Regular family mealtimes Set mealtimes form an important part of your toddler's routine. When you eat with her, she will pick up your good habits, such as how to use cutlery and have good table manners. Even if you can't eat together every day, try to have certain mealtimes each week when you do all sit down to eat together.

Keep it social Resist the temptation to do other jobs while your toddler is busy eating. She loves your company and will behave better if you're around. Avoid eating in front of the television, too—feeding herself is a complicated process and she needs to concentrate on that, not on a television program.

Mealtimes are good opportunities to be social. Help conversation by turning off distractions, such as the television or music, so your toddler can practice the skills of listening and responding.

Around the table If you can, have meals at a table. Sitting upright is good for digestion and makes it easier to use cups and cutlery. Pull the high chair right up to the table so that your toddler is sitting next to you.

Hand control

Intricate play

Your toddler is gaining the dexterity to pick up, examine, twist, and turn the smallest of objects he can find. With this ability comes a burst of satisfaction, and opportunities for more exploration and independence.

How these activities help your toddler

When you introduce your toddler to smaller toys and objects requiring more intricate movements, you're helping him:

★ **Gain fine muscle control.** Your toddler needs practice moving and holding objects with his thumb and forefinger to improve his pincer grip.

★ **Make more precise movements.** With practice, your toddler's grip will be more accurate and his movements smoother.

★ **Do more for himself.** Now he can grasp, turn, and twist objects with finger and thumb, he can open doors, get his toys out, and begin to feed himself more independently.

★ **Increase his range of play.** As he combines his improved dexterity and growing imagination, his play can become more complex.

Pick up, put down Your toddler is able to use her hands and fingers more precisely now, so offer her toys with smaller moving parts appropriate for her age, or supervise her picking up large buttons, or small toys, and moving them between containers.

Sending a letter With more control over how firm or gentle his grasp, your toddler can turn pages in his books one at a time, successfully pop "letters" made from squares of card into a homemade mailbox or use toy paper money when he plays shopping.

KEY FACT
Your baby's abilities work together to improve his skills. For example, as his concentration improves, he is able to focus on increasingly complicated hand movements.

Toys for toddlers

Your toddler is developing rapidly and so his toys need to cater for his ever-expanding skill set.

Challenging toys Introduce new toys with activities that he can almost complete next to some of his old favorites that he finds easy for when he gets frustrated. Your toddler probably won't stick with one game for long, so keep a steady stream of toys and games coming to keep him entertained.

A good mix Try to select toys that add variety to your toddler's play and stimulate different areas of his development. Include toys that increase his active play and mobility, such as tricycles, ride-on toys, and balls to throw and roll. For good play value, and to help with his finer movements and coordination, pick stacking, sorting, and construction toys.

Thinking games Stimulate his thinking and imagination with jigsaws, puppets, sorting toys, play kitchens, and car sets. There are also plenty of toys and games to help his speech and language. Find interactive books to share, mats and instruments to make music, and play phones he can pretend to talk on.

Social play Build his social skills by joining in the play yourself. Take turns at a stuffed animals' tea party—talk as you play with him and follow his lead in the activity rather than directing what he does.

Twist and turn As his wrist and fingers work smoothly together, he'll love complicated toys with knobs to turn and pieces to move and control. Try him with a toddler workbench, music center, or steering wheel to exercise his fingers and his imagination.

Hand control

Marvelous mess

Your tactile toddler will make the most of every messy play experience. He wants to use his fingertips, palms, and all of his hand to dig into, manipulate, and make things with the materials you give him. Join in yourself and you'll understand why this is so appealing!

How these activities help your toddler

When you let your toddler get his hands immersed in messy materials you are helping him:

★ **Use his hands with precision.** Your toddler is figuring out how to build and shape materials to create simple structures such as mud pies.

★ **Experience different sensations.** It is through squeezing, pinching, stirring, pulling, and pressing that your toddler discovers how things feel and respond to his touch.

★ **Stimulate his senses.** He's learning about different textures and consistencies in his messy play.

★ **Play freely.** When he has your permission to make a mess, he can immerse himself in his play without worrying about your reaction.

1 **To make playdough,** gather all your ingredients together: a quarter cup of salt; one cup of flour; and around a quarter cup of water. Put the salt and the flour into a large mixing bowl and then mix them together.

2 **Add water gradually to the dry ingredients**—you'll need around a quarter of a cup or maybe more. Mix together with the spoon as you pour in the water until the mixture starts to develop a doughlike consistency.

3 **Work the dough** into a ball shape inside the bowl, then take it out of the bowl and place it on a hard surface. Start to knead the dough with your knuckles. Give your toddler a smaller bowl so that he can squeeze and knead too.

4 **Roll out the dough**—get your toddler to help with a toy rolling pin. Guide him to cut out shapes using the bottom of cups or fun-shaped cutters. Keep spare dough balls for your toddler to make some figures or animals.

TOP TIP

Messy play is ideal when you have children of different ages to occupy as each can play busily with the same materials at their own level of dexterity and understanding.

Muddy mess Your toddler is using his hands to create, so let him feel the soil on his fingers as he forms a mud pie, digs with you in the garden, or uses his own little watering can to produce a puddle to pat and splash.

(Hand control)

Making a mark

Unleash your toddler's creativity with paint, crayons, and chalk, and you'll be giving her hands and fingers a workout as well. It's quite a challenge for her to hold a brush or chunky crayon, then move it across paper, but the satisfaction of creating those first marks makes it all worthwhile.

How these activities help your toddler

When your toddler has a range of art activities and materials to try you are helping her:

★ **Fine tune control of her hands and fingers.** It takes good small muscle control to make a mark with paint, chalk, or crayons.

★ **Bring large and small movements together.** Your toddler needs good control of both her arms and her hands together to put her crayon to paper.

★ **Explore texture.** As she gets her hands into paint, mud, and sand, your toddler is learning how to hold, squeeze, and move them.

In addition to...

★ **Be creative.** Your toddler's first drawing or painting is the beginning of her expressing and enjoying herself through art.

My hand print Finger paints are a wonderfully messy way for your toddler to explore with her hands. Put out two or three colors, and let her dip right into the paint, then smooth it with abandon on thick sheets of paper, or make hand prints on rolled out wallpaper.

Making bold marks Your toddler can practice his grasp by holding cups of sand as he transfers them to larger buckets or into a sandbox to make castles or shapes. By pressing hard, he can push blocks or stones into mud or wet sand to leave an imprint.

A different angle Once she's steady on her feet, your toddler may find it easier to draw standing at a white board or easel rather than sitting at a table. She can make marks, blobs and bold lines using felt-tip pens or big, easily held paint brushes.

I can draw Her first try at pen control comes with chunky chalk and fat crayons. Help her close her fist around them and scribble on paper. Supervise closely —she hasn't learned yet where it is okay to scribble and places she shouldn't.

Left- and right-handedness

Whether your toddler prefers to use her left or right hand won't be immediately obvious in her first year.

A clear preference In the early months when she's playing or reaching out, your toddler will grab with the hand closest to what she wants, rather than twisting or turning to use a preferred hand. By around 18 months, though, you may start to notice that she favors one hand over the other, and by the age of three her choice will be clear.

A natural choice It's not known how strong an influence parents can play in changing their baby's handedness, but, in general, it's wise to allow this to come naturally. You can expect that if you are right-handed, it is very likely that your children will be, too. Where one or both parents is left-handed, around 50 percent of their children will also be left-handed.

TOP TIP

There is no "right" way to be creative, so genuine praise for all your toddler's efforts, no matter how they look to you, will build her self-esteem and encourage her to do more.

Again and again It can be almost as satisfying to your toddler to wipe off her drawing as it is to make it. Help her with a damp sponge or cloth, and then watch her fill the space again with her next scribble or swirl.

(Communication skills)

Hand signals

Your toddler is really mastering hand signals now. She's learning that small movements and gestures can get her message across and help you understand her needs. The power of her pointing finger to get what she wants or show you something important will motivate her to learn more.

How these activities help your toddler

When you use lots of gestures as you communicate with your toddler and respond to hers, you're helping her:

★ Enrich her message. Gestures give you more information to interpret her words and sounds.

★ Learn the meaning of gestures. As she watches and copies your subtle hand and body movements, she's figuring out what each denotes.

★ Interact with you. Giving and receiving meaning through gestures is part of the two-way nature of communication.

KEY FACT
Studies show that seeing your face when you talk and having lower background noise in the home, for example by reducing TV or radio noise, makes it easier for babies to acquire language.

Point and name Make gestures meaningful by encouraging your toddler to point to the pictures in a book as you name them, or show you where household objects are by pointing.

Clap hands Clapping and patty-cake games involve gestures as part of the rhyme. Teaching her these games shows her another way in which hand signals and gestures can help to convey her message.

How language develops

At around 12 months, your toddler will delight you by saying "mama" or "dada," as her babbling develops into understandable words.

A growing vocabulary By 18 months, your toddler may be using around six to 20 words and gaining more at a rapid rate. Most of these will be naming words such as "milk" and "daddy"; a lesser number will be action words and descriptions, such as "gone," "bye bye," or "more." She may be putting two words together to create simple sentences, such as "Mommy gone," and will use gestures alongside her speech to add meaning or emphasis. Her gestures are also becoming more complex and she's using her gaze to direct your attention to what she wants.

Her favorite word is "no" as she asserts her independence. She will also hold little conversations with herself, mimicking the back and forth of talk using sounds and words.

Your toddler's comprehension At this age, she can understand far more words than she can actually say. She'll respond to simple instructions, such as "no" or "Drink your milk" and will point if you ask her "Where's your tummy?"

Hello, goodbye Show your toddler that she can use waving in different situations. Wave together to see off visitors or to signal "over here" to approaching friends. Pair waving with saying "goodbye" to stuffed animals as they're put away and include it in her play.

Question and answer Teach your toddler different gestures as you talk. Open your hands and shrug as you ask a question, wag your finger side to side for "no," and put up your palms for "stop." She'll soon understand and copy you.

(Communication skills)

I've got rhythm

Your toddler will make music for the joy of it—join him and enjoy yourself too and you'll both get the most out of the experience. Rhythm, rhyme, and movement are rich sources of learning, so make music part of your toddler's play every day.

How these activities help your toddler

When you give your toddler instruments to play and rhymes, music, and songs to share, you are helping him:

★ **Learn the pattern of speech.** Children's rhymes reflect the rhythms of sentences and conversation and help your toddler's language development.

★ **Express himself.** The sounds, dance moves, and actions he makes give him a way to communicate with you without using words.

★ **Copy you.** Your toddler is figuring out how to form sounds and words by looking at your mouth and tongue as you speak. As you share a nursery rhyme face to face, he can watch you closely and learn.

In addition to...

★ **Anticipate what comes next.** The predictable nature of a familiar rhyme or song allows your toddler to think ahead and get excited about what comes next.

Shake and make music With a basket of musical instruments, such as homemade shakers, drums, and maracas, you and your toddler can make some noise. Experiment with different sounds, label noises as soft or loud, and name instruments as you try them.

Natural rhythm Bang out a beat on pots and pans using wooden spoons as drum sticks. Try playing slowly and making a sad face, then fast and looking excited or happy to help your toddler learn that music can communicate mood.

Strumming Your baby will enjoy plucking at or brushing his fingers over the strings of a children's guitar to make a variety of sounds. This activity allows him to combine his love of music with his ability to coordinate his fine hand movements.

Rhymes and repetition Nursery rhymes are rich with opportunities to communicate. Sing her favorites like "Twinkle, twinkle little star" or "Itsy bitsy spider" again and again and she'll follow the verses and anticipate each action with excitement.

How music affects development

There is no doubt that babies and toddlers naturally enjoy listening and moving to music and songs. Other than this simple enjoyment, the benefits of music to your toddler's development are clear when it comes to how he communicates with others and expresses himself.

Words and rhythm Songs and rhymes help build her vocabulary; teach her the patterns and rhythm of speech; and involve waiting and listening, which is central to smooth communication.

Mood music Listening to songs and music has a noticeable influence on your toddler's mood and reaction. When he was a baby, he might have fallen asleep to your lullabies or humming. Now, as a toddler, he may be calmed by soft, slow music or energized by a strong beat or a lively marching song.

Communication There's a social element to music and singing. Your toddler will build relationships through sharing action rhymes, and by dancing or playing musical games with you, or with other toddlers at playgroup.

Benefits for older children It is unclear whether music improves brain development overall for toddlers, since studies with this age group are lacking. However, the benefit of music to development in children three and above is more clear. Some research shows advantages, such as increased mathematical skills and better awareness of space and dimensions, when children are regularly exposed to music.

Fun with music Making music for the pure enjoyment of it is what motivates your toddler. Give him a selection of instruments and he'll find a favorite.

157

(Brain power)

What does this do?

Your inquisitive toddler is finding out how things fit together, come apart, fall, and balance. She needs to repeat tasks again and again, so let her keep trying, even when you can see she has an almost impossible mission.

How these activities help your toddler

When you let your toddler explore and experiment with how things work, you are helping her:

★ Figure out categories. Your toddler is beginning to see how things group together and is understanding different types of objects.

★ Get the idea of representation. Your toddler is realizing that toys represent real objects and she can play with them as versions of their life-size counterpart.

★ Understand the properties of objects. She's experimenting with size, gravity, balance, and other concepts to build her understanding of how things work.

Fitting in Your toddler is just beginning to understand how objects can be bigger or smaller than each other. Offer a variety of simple lift-out puzzles and nesting cubes to help her figure out how things fit together.

Cause and effect Your toddler loves to make things happen. Give pop-up toys or activity centers that give feedback, with boxes that open or lights that go on—he'll notice that his actions produce a reaction.

Make a connection Your toddler is starting to group toys and see connections. Help him sort sets of toys, such as cars or animals, and put parts together to make a whole, perhaps attaching train cars.

Build it up Your toddler wants to know how things connect, stack, and fall. Offer blocks for construction and stacking toys. He's ready to build towers and enjoy the effect when he knocks them down.

Just like the real thing Your toddler's play shows that she's made the connection between objects in the world and her toy versions. She'll push her car on a track, tuck a teddy bear into bed, or "cook" in a pot.

Brain power

Sorting by size

Your young scientist is ready to experiment—she's finding out about the concepts of size, shape, and position through her play. It will take persistence to grasp these ideas, and you can expect frustration as she learns through trial and error.

How these activities help your toddler

When you give your toddler games and toys that involve the concepts of shape, size, and positioning you are helping her:

★ Understand concepts about physical relationships, necessary to everyday life; even simple instructions such as "Get me the big teddy bear" or "Put the cup on the table" require her to understand these ideas.

★ Discover through experience. Trial-and-error learning is a powerful method as your toddler is learning through her own problem-solving.

★ Deal with her sense of frustration, for example, when to begin with she can't find the right shape to fit into the sorter.

TOP TIP

Art and messy play present ideal opportunities to introduce the concept of size. As your toddler creates, talk about her big or little marks on the paper, or her small and large sand castles.

Build it up Big blocks make it easier to see and feel size differences. There is a sense of satisfaction as she creates a stack and gets the idea of big, bigger, and biggest. Don't interfere, just encourage, as she uses trial and error to figure out that her tower will be steadier with the larger blocks at the bottom.

Brain power

Imagine that

Your toddler's imagination is about to take flight as she begins to act out what she sees and hears. She'll copy what you do, change character through dressing up, and show her tender side as she tucks in her bear.

How these activities help your toddler

Imaginative play is tons of fun for your toddler, but it has a learning element too. It helps her to:

★ **Exercise her imagination.** This is known to increase her creativity, which in turn helps with problem solving as she grows older.

★ **Get plenty of practice with concepts** such as in and out, open and closed, and over and under as she uses her play kitchen or work bench and pretends to feed her stuffed animals.

★ **Begin her understanding of social roles.** As she acts out familiar scenes from home, she's figuring out how the important adults in her life relate to each other.

★ **Identify with you as she copies your behavior.** In the process she's also discovering that she is her own person, separate from you.

★ **Feel close to you.** As she "helps" you around the home with her play version of your chores, this strengthens the bond between you.

Hello? Encourage play and communication by replying when your toddler acts out using the phone. You could also pretend to be his favorite relative answering the call.

Who am I? By popping on a different hat or donning a costume, your toddler is someone new. When she's ready, read a story that relates to her character.

Anyone for dinner? Your toddler is driven to copy what you do. Let her loose in a corner with pots and pans, act out shopping with a basket, and play food, or help her put a stuffed animal in a toy stroller.

Brain power

Where is it?

Your toddler's curiosity is a driving force. She needs to know what happens when toys fall, shift or can't be seen, so she can predict how they'll move. This information is used to create mental maps to make sense of her world.

Search strategy Your toddler understands that likely hiding places are in, under, and behind things, and starts her search there. Conceal toys or action figures in nesting toys or empty cereal packages and give her the task of finding them all.

How these activities help your toddler

Give your toddler hiding games and activities that involve the concepts of "in," "under," "through," and "behind" and you're helping her:

★ **Plan her actions.** Your toddler is learning from experience and actively problem solving. Now she'll search under or behind objects for a hidden toy, rather than simply look around.

★ **Be aware of size and space.** As your toddler tries to push a card through an opening, she's refining her knowledge of the concepts "in," "out," and "through."

★ **Learn the properties of objects.** Your toddler is learning how objects behave. She is realizing that a toy doesn't simply disappear—it falls in a predictable way and takes up space, for example, creating a bulge if covered by a cloth.

Look, feel, and find Put toys and everyday items under a dish towel and encourage your toddler to look then feel with her hands to discover what they are. Ask her about each object saying "Is it a car?" or "Is it a block?" then name it as she reveals it.

TOP TIP
While it's important not to stifle your toddler's curiosity, you need to ensure that she plays safely. Keep hide-and-seek games in one room so you can supervise as she explores.

Brain power

Building memory

Your toddler is using his "working" memory to hold instructions and pass information for permanent storage into his long-term memory. You'll see his memory in action as he remembers where a toy or room is located.

How these activities help your toddler

When you give instructions that are simple, use familiar words, include his name and point as you speak, you are helping him:

★ **Use his "working" memory.** The more clues and cues you give your toddler, the better he's able to hold an instruction in his working memory, then do as you ask.

★ **Use his long-term memory.** When you repeat the same instruction, activity, or routine over and over, you help your toddler store information permanently in his long-term memory.

★ **Create a map.** His mental map is growing as your toddler learns the layout of your home and yard and recognizes the route to favorite places, such as the park.

In addition to...

★ **Get into a routine.** When you ask your toddler to get his hat at the same time every day, he gets to know what is expected of him.

Bring it here Give your toddler's memory a workout by asking her to find familiar toys. For example, say "Please find your teddy." She'll need to remember where it's kept and find that place to complete your instruction.

Finding his way Help your toddler learn the layout of his home. Go on a treasure hunt—ask him to lead you to the bedroom, bathroom, or shed to find hidden toys. Name rooms and describe what they're used for.

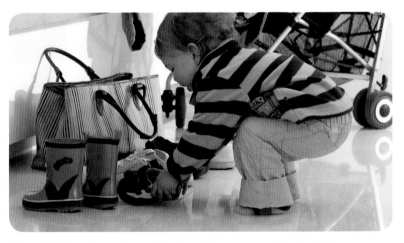

Where is it? Your independent toddler is ready for some practical tasks. Ask him to give you his shoes or hat as a routine when you go out. Repeat the same words each time and make sure the item is always in the same place for him to find.

A toddler memory book

Your toddler's first years pass quickly and probably in a blur of activity. Capture these early memories for both of you through journals, photographs, recordings, and treasured mementos.

For your toddler Your toddler is fascinated with himself and will love to look at photographs, recordings, and mementos of the things he's done. Make him a memory book so he can flick through it himself—it'll need to be robust since he may not handle it carefully. Put in copies of photographs of him, close family and friends, and places he's been. Slip in certificates from his baby swim classes or playgroup, and his own hand- and foot prints.

Memories for you You can create a precious store of memories by collecting objects that remind you of your toddler. Use a special box to save his first shoes, a plaster impression of his hands, his first scribble, and mementos from early vacations. Keep a journal going in the toddler years, put in photographs, and write his milestones and funny things he said or did. As you and your toddler look through them in the years to come, they will bring this time vividly to mind.

Find it Your toddler is learning that many objects have a purpose. Build this into your instructions by asking her to find the cup or bowl for a doll's tea party or her snack time. Help her out the first few times you ask.

19 months to 2 years

YOUR ACTIVE TODDLER

As your toddler approaches two years old, her personality really starts to shine. Her involvement in her world grows, both socially and practically, as she learns to play in bigger groups and manages ever more complex play.

YOUR SOCIAL BABY

Your toddler is on the go constantly and needs to be occupied with plenty of play, both indoors and outside. As her confidence and social ability grow, she'll be increasingly comfortable in the company of other children and will enjoy playgroup environments, which also help keep her well stimulated. You may notice too that she becomes more social generally, and happy to talk to other adults she meets.

As your toddler reaches two years old, you'll recognize complex emotions, such as anxiety and determination in her expression and body language, but she won't be able to name these. You'll notice the emergence of tantrums from 16 months of age onward, as anger and frustration sweep through her, causing her to lose control. Tantrums also arise when she feels unable to get her meaning across, and they're her favorite method to show her annoyance when you say "no." Being aware of when she's tired or hungry and more likely to be overwrought, and avoiding potential conflict at these times, helps to minimize outbursts. In contrast, you'll notice a caring side emerge, often expressed in role play, for example as she tucks her stuffed animals into bed.

GETTING MOVING

As your toddler begins to run, jump, climb, and kick, it's balance that she needs. This involves input from what she sees, feedback from her muscles, and information from the vestibular, or "balancing," system in the inner ear telling her that she is moving or stopping. Her brain is working overtime to understand all these signals and how they fit together, and it is through plenty of big play that this comes about. Swings, slides, trampolines, seesaws, jumping, and bouncing all give her experience of these three sets of signals working together.

Once her balance is more established and she's confident walking and running, she'll experience the thrill of climbing and, by the time she's two years old, she'll kick a ball.

HAND CONTROL

As your baby approaches two years old, her hand control will be more refined. She'll be turning the page of her books, managing large buttons and Velcro fastenings, and making her mark with crayon or brush. Where at first she held crayons in a fist, by the end of her second year she may be using a "tripod" grip with her thumb and two fingers. Furthermore, increased flexibility in her wrist means that her drawing can evolve as she manages to move the crayon or brush in different directions. Her greater hand–eye coordination also means that her aim is significantly improved now and she may start to throw a ball roughly in the direction she intends, or she'll use a wooden hammer to bang pegs into holes. Sticky bricks, construction toys, and building blocks start to be of more interest as she learns to fit pieces together and has the steadiness to build towers of several blocks.

COMMUNICATION SKILLS

From her first attempts to get her message across by crying, through to using gurgles, babbles, first words and two-word sentences, she has gradually found her voice and will enjoy your reaction to it. By two years old, she may have a vocabulary of around 200 words and will put two or more words together to make simple sentences such as "Want milk." She'll gain words more quickly the more you speak to her.

Increasingly social Throughout this second year, your toddler will grow more accustomed to playing alongside others.

Perfectly poised Once your toddler's balance is established, he'll manage actions that require steadiness and concentration.

Her understanding of more complex ideas is also coming along quickly, and as she reaches two years, she'll be able to obey some simple requests such as "Bring me the cup," or will assert herself and decide not to do it at all!

From 19 months, she'll add even more gestures to illustrate her point; usually these arm and hand movements are copied directly from you.

BRAIN POWER

Her new discovery is the notion that things have properties, such as color or size, and can be the same or different. Between 19 months and two years, she'll enjoy matching and pairing games as this understanding grows. She'll also enjoy more challenging puzzles and jigsaws as her problem-solving skills improve. Her logic is developing too, but she may not always attribute the right reason to why something happens.

By her second year, her involvement in imaginary worlds grows. She identifies with characters in a story, showing an interest in what happens to them, and plays "pretend" by dressing up or acting out with dolls and play figures. Beware, you may see signs of yourself in her imaginary play as she'll love to act out familiar scenes of family life.

Different worlds Your toddler will immerse himself in pretend worlds over the course of his second year. Farm sets, train tracks, and other miniature worlds will delight him and teach him many new things about the real world.

Good control Your toddler's grip is becoming more adultlike as he uses his thumb and first fingers to manage his play.

On the go Your busy toddler will like nothing more than racing around on tricycles, first scooters, or toy tractors. Giving him plenty of time outside and fun outdoor equipment will keep him active, happy, and full of energy.

Act it out

Your young performer is ready to explore social relationships in her fantasy play. She's trying out the words, actions, and interactions she sees around her. Your toddler is a sharp observer and she may mimic your tone or mannerisms to the delight of those watching.

How these activities help your toddler

When you give your toddler plenty of props for her pretend play you are helping her:

★ **Develop her social skills.** Imaginative play allows your child to try out social behaviors before she has to use them in real life situations.

★ **Build her understanding of others.** It is a sign of your toddler's increasing empathy with others that she can observe, then act out, caring behavior.

★ **Experiment with different social roles.** As she plays at parenting her toys, your toddler is trying on this role and gaining understanding of herself and others.

★ **Enjoy time with you.** At first, your toddler will want to include you in her pretend play. As she reaches two years old, she'll love you to be her audience.

Dinner time Your toddler's imaginative play will be centered on familiar scenes, such as mealtimes. Give her plastic cups and plates so she can arrange a teddy bears' picnic, or suggest holding a pizza party for all her action figures.

Cosy up Being enveloped, hidden, or covered can be appealing to your toddler, and he'll enjoy getting into his "home" of a large cardboard box, or a draped sheet over the table. Once inside, he's ready to play with his family of toys.

Routines Your toddler will want her toys to take part in a routine like her own. You may be surprised how well she copies what you say and do as she puts her toys to bed or gives them a bath in the sink.

Relationships You may notice your toddler treating his toys to instructions such as "Stop it" or "Go" in a tone very like your own. He'll act out other scenarios too, holding toys face to face as they "talk" to each other.

TOP TIP

In addition to helping develop creativity and social understanding, "let's pretend" scenarios, including imaginary friends, are also thought to help children deal with stressful situations.

Caring times As her understanding of other people begins, your toddler will act out caring rituals. Give her toys that help her play this out, such as dolls or stuffed animals to cradle, baby bottles for feeding, and a crib or stroller for her to tuck toys into.

Your social baby

Miniature worlds

Your toddler is exercising his imagination on his "miniature" worlds. He's giving voice and action to toy people and animals, and to himself when he dresses up. All this helps him learn about behavior and relationships.

How these activities help your toddler

With a toy box of figures, animals, farm and zoo sets and a dressing-up box of simple costumes, your toddler is:

★ **Developing his concept of representation.** As your toddler gives voice and action to his toy figures, he is assigning them social qualities and using them to represent "real" people.

★ **Trying out new behaviors.** Dressing up gives your toddler the opportunity to experiment with a different persona and exaggerate his voice and actions.

★ **Watching and copying others.** Through observing the imaginative play of older children, your toddler has the opportunity to copy more complex ideas and scenarios.

Mini me Your toddler is starting to use play figures to represent herself and the wider family. As she reaches two years old, she will enjoy putting them in their place in her dolls' house, bus, or car.

TOP TIP
Encouraging role play can help your toddler's emotional development since it provides a forum for him to act out emotions that he may find hard to verbalize.

Joining in Older children who are more experienced in imaginary play can involve your toddler in their activities. As they move figures and make animal noises with a farm or zoo set, your toddler will observe and copy.

Try it on As his interest in dressing up grows, help your toddler into costumes of animals and characters he's seen in books or television programs. Talk with him as if he is the character he's dressed as, or read him a story about the character.

Your social baby

Run off, come back

He may be more independent, but your toddler needs you nearby when he ventures off—your presence allows him to concentrate and feel safe. He'll catch your eye, call out, or come over to check that you're still there.

Watch me play Your toddler is ready to go off to the sandbox or play with a basket of toys across the room when you are around. She's growing more secure: if she can see you when she looks up, or knows you will come if she calls, she'll usually play happily.

How these activities help your toddler

When you stay nearby and keep a close eye on your toddler while he plays you are helping him:

★ Feel confident to go off to play. His attachment to you is still strong, but now your toddler can hold a comforting image of you in his mind, which allows him to leave your side to play.

★ Use you as a secure base. Your toddler needs to be able to see or touch you every so often to reassure himself that you are still there for him.

★ Concentrate on having fun. When he is sure you are looking out for him, your toddler can throw himself into his play rather than being watchful himself.

Near and far In the yard or at the park, your toddler may be happy to play within sight or, if he's tired or unsettled, stay close by. It's common to be changeable in how independent or clingy he is.

Are you there? When you touch base with your toddler while he plays, by catching his eye, waving, or going over to comment on or praise what he's doing, he's reminded that you're keeping him in mind.

Getting moving

Introducing ball games

Your active toddler has started to run, jump, and kick, exercising his new found coordination. Ball games give him the perfect opportunity to enjoy playtime with you and sharpen these emerging physical skills.

How these activities help your toddler

By playing throwing, rolling, or kicking ball games, you're helping your toddler:

★ Balance. Shifting his weight onto one foot when he kicks, or leaning his body to throw, improves his stability.

★ Work on his hand–eye coordination. He's using information from his eyes and feedback from his muscles to improve the accuracy of his throw.

★ Refine his use of his body. He's using his muscles to apply force and start a trajectory as he makes the ball move.

In addition to...

★ Play games. Ball games are social, involving cooperation and turn taking.

Aim it Get your toddler hitting with a large foam bat or lightweight racket. Toddler basketball or bowling games help his aim. Each time he aims at the ball, hoop, or bowling pins, his coordination develops.

Kick it His first kicks will be more of a shove with the foot than a full strike. Keep your toddler trying with a big beach ball and a small soccer goal for a target, or play the part of goalkeeper and get him to aim toward you.

How girls and boys play

Whether your toddler is a boy or a girl, he or she will get great satisfaction and pleasure from all the running, jumping, and climbing involved in active play. At the moment, it's really too early to notice particular gender differences during play, although these may emerge later.

Early differences When you compare your child with a peer of the opposite sex, you may notice some variety in their play and development. This is a natural result of being distinct individuals, rather than an effect of gender differences. At this age, boys and girls tend to be as curious, active, and playful as each other, and differences stem from their own unique personality and preferences, rather than their sex or your influence as a parent.

As children grow Differences in physical play between boys and girls will emerge, however, as your child gets older. From around three onward, studies have shown that boys typically start to engage in more rough and tumble play than girls. In their imaginative play, girls are more likely to act out common household scenarios, while boys favor copying favorite characters from books and television.

Throw it Soft balls and bean bags with a fabric tail that are easy to handle encourage your toddler to throw, bounce, and roll. Start by practicing his throwing skills with him; catching will come later on.

Getting moving

Action play

Your intrepid climber wants to get up and go. She's enjoying her increased strength, coordination, and ability to use equipment to lift off and move. Enjoy her pleasure as she rides, bounces, climbs, and slides.

How these activities help your toddler

With playground trips and equipment that invite your toddler to move, slide, jump, and climb, you're helping her:

★ Use big muscles groups. Big movements and active play increase strength and coordination in the muscles of the trunk, shoulders, legs, and arms.

★ Improve her awareness of space. As she moves down a slide or tips over and rights herself, she's adjusting herself to move through different dimensions.

★ Enjoy movement. The thrill of flying through the air, bouncing up, and sliding down is joyful for your toddler.

Up and down Your toddler's balance is improving and she'll be able to walk up and down stairs with a helping hand or supervision from you. Count each step she takes to give her a sense of achievement.

Swing up Your toddler feels like she's flying when you gently hold her arms and swing her between you. She'll quickly get into the rhythm of stepping and lifting off as you walk along together.

Bounce, bounce Now your toddler is able to squat and stand up, she's got the moves to jump on any springy surface. A bed or sofa is ideal for bouncing, but you'll need to decide whether this is how you want your furniture used!

Climb up, slide down The slide may become your toddler's favorite for the thrill it gives her. Her muscles are working to keep her upright and stop herself at the bottom, but she won't notice as she revels in the slipping and sliding.

Jump up Being able to jump with both feet together means that your toddler can get bouncing on his hold-on trampoline. The hand rail will give him the stability to jump higher, with the confidence that he can keep his balance.

Push off Riding toys and tricycles are a great way for your toddler to get around. He's not ready to peddle yet, but will push himself along with both feet together at first, then start alternating them in a walking motion.

Being an active family

Your toddler loves to be active, but he'll enjoy it even more if the whole family gets involved.

Making the effort It can be difficult to fit active play into home life, yet almost three-quarters of families report that they would like to do more physical activity together.

Daily activity The answer is to find small opportunities each day to get moving. You don't need to go out for the day or run around for hours to get the benefit of being active. Experts say that just 15 minutes of active family play every day makes a difference to children being a healthy weight, and that children should have at least 60 minutes of play a day, including the "family play," in total.

Quick indoor games Play with balloons by batting them to each other or use hands and feet to keep them from touching the floor. Enjoy dancing to a CD, or play follow the leader, or a game of hide-and-seek.

Outdoor activities Try a treasure hunt; blow then try to catch bubbles as they float away; play tag, but go slowly enough that your toddler can catch you; and try throwing or kicking games outside. Whenever possible, go farther afield to the park or walk the dog together.

Eyes and hands together

Your toddler's improved hand–eye coordination and increased control of the fine muscles of his hands and fingers help him to explore objects and toys with an increased precision and aim.

How these activities help your toddler

When you keep your toddler's hands busy with games and activities that require small movements and accuracy, you are helping him:

★ **Work his eyes and hands together.** The precision of his fine movements is still developing and relies on feedback from what he sees and feels.

★ **Develop his aim.** Your toddler knows how his arm moves and swings without looking at it, but needs to focus on the target to improve his aim.

★ **Explore by touch.** When he can touch but not see what he's doing, your toddler must rely on past experience of how his hands move to guide him.

In addition to...

★ **Match sound and action.** Your toddler is learning to predict the sound that goes with an action. His knowledge of sounds allows him to anticipate who or what is approaching by their noise.

Pull apart Scrunching and unfolding tissue, opening an envelope, or tearing layers of paper as he opens a present, make a satisfying sound and require his eyes and hands to work together efficiently.

Bang and hammer Your toddler is ready to aim and swing with a hammer. He'll enjoy banging in pegs, knocking balls down a hole, playing notes on a xylophone, or hammering away at his workbench.

Feel it Put different toys and objects into a cloth bag for your toddler. As he looks at the bumps in the cloth and puts in his hand to explore varying textures and shapes with his fingers, tell him the name of each object.

Dig down Her sensitive finger tips are working hard as your toddler digs to find animals buried in the sandbox, dives in to find a prize in a homemade treasure chest, or digs behind sofa cushions for a hidden toy.

Hand control

Small moves

Your toddler wants to help herself and will get great satisfaction from accomplishing practical tasks such as pulling off a sock, undoing a strap, or finally fitting a puzzle piece. She's combining fine motor skills and problem-solving abilities to make these intricate movements possible.

How these activities help your toddler

Toys and activities that demand fine movements with small pieces help her:

★ **Practice precise movements.** Rotating, pulling, and slotting in large buttons, zip pulls, or puzzle pieces improves muscle control and maneuvering.

★ **Problem solve.** To get a puzzle piece to fit into its hole, your toddler must understand the task, plan for it, and persist in trying.

★ **Become more independent.** Doing more for herself means being able to apply her manual dexterity to play and everyday tasks.

Get it on Whether she's putting her hand into the sleeve of her coat as you hold it open, pulling up a sock, or pulling her t-shirt down, your toddler is putting her dexterity to practical use in dressing.

Open and close At first your toddler will find removing clothes easier than putting them on. Guide his hand to pull the Velcro open on his shoe or grasp and pull down a big zipper tag to unfasten his coat.

Fit in Lift-out puzzles and two- or six-piece wooden jigsaws help your toddler with precise grasp and maneuvering pieces. In a few months, she'll use her pincer grip and improve accuracy to thread giant beads.

Dress up Your toddler gets pleasure and fine tunes her movements when she dresses and takes care of her dolls, puts equipment on action figures, or plays with toys designed to teach her how to do fastenings.

Complex play The intricate hand and finger movements required to open and manipulate small windows and doors and position furniture in a dolls' house, is great practice for your toddler's coordination.

Hand control

Getting creative

Your toddler's creativity is beginning to blossom. Foster her artistic interests with a craft box bulging with supplies, and find the time to make things together. She'll reap the benefits in improved coordination, increased creativity, and satisfaction.

Cut it up Teach your toddler to use first scissors by guiding her fingers into the holes, then practice opening and closing movements with your hand over hers. With your help, she'll love to snip at stiff paper or play dough.

Make it big Being creative in three dimensions using play dough, papier mâché, or scrunched up tissue paper gets your toddler using her hands to build shapes into her first sculpture.

Dab it For a quick and easy art activity, give your toddler a sponge and several saucers of paint, demonstrate how to get just enough paint on the sponge, then dab or streak it onto paper.

Stick it on Collect up images from magazines and old cards for your toddler to create her first collage. Use cardboard for backing and apply the glue stick together as she arranges the pictures to her satisfaction.

How these activities help your toddler

Cutting, gluing, sticking, modeling, and painting all help your toddler:

★ Exercise her fine motor skills. As the small muscles of her hands and fingers develop, her movements will be smoother and more controlled.

★ Try new movements. The opening and closing motion of scissors presents a new challenge in control and coordination for hands and fingers.

★ Use different materials. Your toddler is finding out the subtle differences in how to handle things that are hard, soft, sloppy, or flimsy.

In addition to …

★ Make something. Having something to hold, look at and show to others for her effort is satisfying and a boost to your toddler's self-esteem.

TOP TIP
Glue, paint, and dough can all be messy. Containing the chaos with a designated arts and crafts area helps you to relax and allows your toddler to enjoy "unrestricted" messy play time.

(Hand control)

I'll do it

Concentration, coordination, and control of fine movements go into your toddler's efforts to help himself. He's ready to put movements together to achieve simple tasks, from opening doors to washing his face.

How these activities help your toddler

By giving your toddler opportunities to be independent and try more complex tasks, you are helping him:

★ **Put together intricate movements to complete a task.** Most practical activities require a sequence of coordinated movements and these take lots of practice to perfect.

★ **Make adjustments in his grasp.** Within each task, your toddler must recognize the need to loosen and tighten his grip as the activity demands.

★ **Satisfy your toddler's drive to do things for himself.** As his dexterity and coordination improve, so will his ability to take care of himself.

Open and shut As your toddler gains the strength and control to grip and turn knobs, she'll be able to open doors, cupboards, and latches. Encourage this ability, because it allows her more freedom to explore.

TOP TIP

Boost your toddler's self-esteem by helping him achieve some simple initial tasks. Discovering that he can succeed will give him the confidence to try again.

Wash it Your toddler has the coordination to help as you wash her. Give her a washcloth or sponge to soak and rub on her face and body; encourage her by naming each body part as she washes it.

Clean up Start him on the rubbing and turning motions he needs to wash his hands. He's grasping and twisting at each stage as he turns on the faucet, applies soap to his palms, and rubs them under the water.

The emergence of tantrums

What is labeled the "terrible twos" can start as early as 16 months. When your toddler reaches a stage called "differentiation," he recognizes he is actually separate from you and able to make his own choices.

First tantrums As he struggles to assert himself, it's normal to have tantrums at least once a day. These are an expression of strong emotions, when your toddler doesn't know how to communicate his feelings in words. You'll notice they are often triggered by frustration, having to share, and being told. "no". They're more likely when he is hungry, tired, or overstimulated.

Prevention tactics Reduce the chance of a tantrum by redirecting your child's attention if you see a storm brewing. Timing helps too—schedule activities that have a high tantrum risk, such as a supermarket trip, at times when your toddler is well fed and rested.

Dealing with tantrums When a tantrum does erupt, take your toddler out of the situation to a quiet spot and wait for him to calm down. Strong emotions can be scary, so stay near him and stay calm. Don't try to reason with your toddler until the tantrum is over and he is settled enough to listen.

Put it on Make it simple for your toddler to put on his shoes by starting with slip-ons or simple sandals. Sit him down and, if necessary, steady him with a hand on his shoulder as he tries to balance, hold the shoe, and poke in his toe.

Communication skills

More talk

The more you talk together, the chattier your toddler will be. Repeat back a clearer version of what she said, guess her meaning and comment on what's happening. She'll amaze you with how much she understands.

How these activities help your toddler

With chitchat at every opportunity you are helping your toddler:

★ Build sentences. When your toddler puts two words together, then hears you expand on it, she is learning how to construct a sentence.

★ Explain herself. Your toddler is increasingly using words to express what she wants; your reaction tells her that she's on the right track and encourages her to keep trying.

★ Have a conversation. Your toddler is learning the give and take of speaking and listening that is essential to talking.

In addition to...

★ Gain social skills. As she joins in and listens to family chatter, she is practicing being social and showing an interest in others.

More language As your toddler progresses to two-word sentences, expand on each idea by extending the sentence. For example if he asks "Me in?" develop it into "Do you want to go in?" or says "My car," reply "It's a car, thank you for the car."

Chatter box Give your toddler practice at holding a conversation. Sit opposite each other so she can see your face and hands, ask her what she's been doing and wait for her to answer with a word or gesture. Nod and reply to keep the talking going.

Talk at mealtimes When you share information at mealtimes, you're setting up a habit that will ensure long-term family communication. Keep it simple: ask and talk about what's happened that day, and plan what you'll do next.

KEY FACT
A recent study highlighted two-way parent–child conversation as the ideal way to develop language. Reading and speaking often to your child and reducing TV time were also important.

Communication skills

Book power

Get your toddler into the reading habit by including books in her daily routine. You're her narrator, so give it all you've got: use different voices, expressions, gestures, or sound effects to make stories more powerful.

Name it Learning the name of common objects is important to your toddler. So, as you look at picture books together, don't just tell the story—point and name whatever you see as well.

More than words Books with textures or sounds boost your child's learning. When you say "soft" as he touches a fluffy patch, he'll remember the word better. His memory is improved the more senses he uses.

How these activities help your toddler

By reading, looking at picture books and photo albums, acting out stories, and telling jokes you are helping her:

★ Put a name to it. She wants to know the name of everything she sees, and picture books are ideal to teach her.

★ Bring words to life. When your stories name and describe emotions, your toddler is learning to label feelings.

★ Become involved in a story. As she gets to know that stories have a beginning, middle, and conclusion, she'll get lost in the tale and desperate to know what happens.

In addition to...

★ Enjoy time with you. Snuggling up for a bedtime story ends the day with an opportunity for closeness.

Lift and look Use your tone of voice to build the anticipation before your toddler lifts a flap or turns a page. Ask her what she thinks is under the flap and see if she can guess what's next.

My family Looking at photo albums together gives you plenty to talk about. Your toddler will identify current photographs of herself, but may not know which are her baby ones. Talk about the family as you look.

Brain power

What's that?

As your toddler's memory and nervous system mature, she's recognizing greater detail from finer textures to more subtle colors. All the information she gains builds her knowledge of color, sound, texture, tastes, and smells, and she'll recognize them next time.

How these activities help your toddler

When you stimulate all her senses in play, at meals and in quiet moments, you are helping your toddler:

★ **Recognize different surfaces.** Your toddler is building up a store of information about how things feel and react to her touch.

★ **Expand her diet.** It is through repeatedly seeing, feeling, and tasting new foods that your toddler is prepared to swallow them.

★ **Develop her vision.** Your toddler needs to be exposed to lots of visual stimuli for her vision to mature.

Touch it Name the different sensations as she explores surfaces such as rough paper, furry cloth, and kitchen scrubbers. Describe the feeling as she squeezes and prods cotton balls, dough, or cool mashed potato.

KEY FACT

Your child learns with all five senses, so don't underestimate the importance of stimulation. To learn more about her world, she needs an environment that engages all of her senses.

Taste it Your toddler's lips and tongue provide her brain with sensory feedback from whatever she tastes. Give her different flavors and textures to try, such as yogurt, banana, or slices of crunchy apple.

Smell it Smell is a powerful sense that can conjure memories and aid recognition. Your toddler's sense of smell is well developed. Encourage her to experience food through its smell as well as its taste and texture.

See it The area of your toddler's eye most sensitive to color is still maturing, but he can pick out small changes in shade. Choose books and toys with subtle colors so he can observe these variations in tone.

(Brain power)

Same and different

Your toddler is noticing how things match up or differ. This simple, but vital, concept helps him organize the huge amounts of information he receives. The more he practices now, the better this skill will develop.

How these activities help your toddler

When you play matching games with toys, flash cards, blocks, and games you are helping him:

★ **Recognize categories.** Your toddler must learn through repetition and experience what key features help him group things; for example, are they living or not, does it make a noise?

★ **Organize his thoughts.** Grouping helps your toddler think more quickly. When he encounters something new and fits it successfully into a category, he immediately has some idea of its properties because he already knows about that group of objects.

★ **Identify colors.** Keep labeling colors for your toddler as you play and he'll be able to name one or two colors himself in the coming year.

In addition to...

★ **Improve his vocabulary.** The more you name what your toddler can see, the better his speech development.

Which picture? Play games of naming and pairing members of different categories, such as animals or food, using flash cards. Or introduce "Snap" to make matching fun. Play slowly because she's only just gaining this skill.

Matching up Your toddler can now group objects on her own, but categories may be broad, for example all vehicles may be "car." Work on this with matching games, such as finding two pigs, or the lions in a zoo set.

Color pairs Bricks and blocks make great sorting toys. Give your toddler the challenge of making a tower using the yellow blocks, or pile the blue ones in his dump truck. Put the first one in yourself to make it easier.

Brain power

Piecing it together

Your toddler is applying problem-solving skills to all aspects of his life from playing to feeding and dressing. He's ready to apply previously learned skills on how things fit together to solve more complex puzzles and games.

Fit the pieces Put out a variety of chunky jigsaws for your toddler. As he twists, turns, or forces pieces in, he's applying his problem-solving skills. Let him try on his own first, then gently guide him if necessary.

Shape sorting It's a matter of trial and error as your toddler completes a shape sorter or fits together nesting cups. She may try out each puzzle piece in every slot before she finds the right one.

How these activities help your toddler

By providing a wide range of puzzles, jigsaws, and shape sorters that challenge your toddler's thinking and dexterity you are helping him:

★ Solve practical problems. As your toddler plays with his puzzles, he is using his understanding of space and shape to plan, then try out, how to fit things together.

★ Learn through trial and error. By trying different ways to fit puzzles together, your toddler is figuring out which is the most successful method.

★ Keep trying. It is through using similar problem-solving strategies, no matter which puzzle he tries, that your toddler consolidates his learning.

In addition to...

★ Develop his hand–eye coordination. Guiding jigsaw pieces and shaped blocks into their correct place means that your toddler's eyes and hands must work well together.

Stack it up Your toddler will handle and look at the pieces of a stacking puzzle intently to see if he can figure out how they fit before he places them together. He may need to make several attempts before he's finished.

Useful resources

BREAST-FEEDING

La Leche League

Information and support about breast-feeding

www.lllusa.org

Womenshealth.gov

Information on why breast-feeding is important and tips on making it easier

www.womenshealth.gov/breastfeeding

HEALTH & DEVELOPMENT

US Department of Education—Office of Special Education and Rehabilitative Services

Provides leadership to achieve full integration and participation in society of people with disabilities

www.ed.gov/about/offices/list/osers

All Kinds of Minds

Ideas and tools to spark better learning in public schools and beyond

www.allkindsofminds.org

American Academy of Allergy Asthma and Immunology

Up-to-date information on allergies, asthma, and immunology

www.aaaai.org

American Dietetic Association website for kids

Source for scientifically based health and nutrition information

www.eatright.org/kids

American Speech-Language-Hearing Association

Supports speech-language pathologists, audiologists, and speech, language, and hearing scientists

www.asha.org

Autism Speaks

Dedicated to raising public awareness about autism and its effects on individuals, families, and society. Also provides information on family services.

www.autismspeaks.org

C.H.A.D.D—Children and Adults with Attention Deficit Disorders

Serves individuals with AD/HD and their families

www.chadd.org

Food Allergy and Anaphylaxis Network

Source of information, programs, and resources related to food allergy and anaphylaxis

www.foodallergy.org

Healthy Children—AAP website for parents

Parenting website for information on attaining optimal physical, mental, and social health and well-being for infants, children, and adolescents

www.healthychildren.org

Juvenile Diabetes Research Foundation

Information and support for parents with children who have diabetes

www.jdrf.org

March of Dimes

Works for stronger, healthier babies before and after birth

www.marchofdimes.com

My Child without Limits

Advice and support for parents of children with special needs

www.mychildwithoutlimits.org

National Eczema Association

Advice and information about children with eczema

www.nationaleczema.org

NEW MOTHERS

Mothers and more

Grassroots organization allowing mothers to connect with other new mothers

www.mothersandmore.org

Premature Baby/Premature Child

Supports parents with premature babies by providing information on prematurity and care of babies

www.prematurity.org

GENERAL

American Academy of Pediatrics

General child health information and specific guidelines concerning pediatric issues

www.aap.org

Centers for Disease Control (CDC)

Protects health through prevention of disease, injury, and disability; Provides preparedness plans for new health threats

www.cdc.gov

Consumer Product Safety Commission

Includes information about recalls and safety standards for most children's products

www.cpsc.gov

National Institutes of Health (NIH)

The US's medical research agency

www.nih.gov

National Institute of Mental Health (NIMH)

Works to transform understanding and treatment of mental illnesses through research—paving the way for prevention, recovery, and cure

www.nimh.nih.gov

Index

Acknowledgments

AUTHOR'S ACKNOWLEDGMENTS:

I would like to thank my parents Patricia and George Higginbotham for all their love and in particular my mother who wished this book had been around when I was little. Thanks also to my family Michael, Rupert, Dominic and Toby, to Vicki McIvor for all her work on my behalf, and all at DK who made this book possible and a pleasure to write.

PUBLISHER'S ACKNOWLEDGMENTS:

DK would like to thank Sara Kimmins for the initial idea and styling of books in the series; Becky Alexander for proofreading; Vanessa Bird for the index; Jo Godfrey-Wood for assistance at photo shoots; Victoria Barnes and Roisin Donaghy for hair and makeup; Carly Churchill, the photographer's assistant, and our models: Nina and Anjani Acharya; Stephanie and Thomas Barrington; Kirsty and Kate Campbell; Sarah and Lisa Crowe and Luca Sodeau; Ruth Davies and Florence Knowles; Bea de Lemos and Alexander Walker; Giovanna Franchina and Leonardo Diallo; Shuna Frood and Joe Sutcliffe; Natasha Garry and Solstice River Davies; Oriel Gavin and Erin Smith; Susie and Poppy Howe; Kate Jones and Holly Dixon; Sophie Lewis and Somerset Young; Clare Moore and Cassius Cockrell; Victoria and Max Perrot; Michelle and Edward Phillips; Dawn Robinson and Alexander Whillock; Kate Wheeler and Freya Bartlett; Justyna and Nicole Zohreh; Karolina and Khemilya Ubor; and Alice and Sam Pickles.

The publisher would like to thank the following for their kind permission to reproduce their photographs:

(Key: a-above; b-below/bottom; c-center; l-left; r-right; t-top)

11 Mother & Baby Picture Library: Ian Hooton (bl, br). **13 Corbis:** David Raymer (tr). **Getty Images:** Frank Herholdt (br). **17 Corbis:** Tim Pannell (bl). **18 Corbis:** Larry Williams (c). **Mother & Baby Picture Library:** Ian Hooton (bc); Paul Mitchell (br). **23 SuperStock:** Age Fotostock (cr). **24 Getty Images:** Dennie Cody (br). **29 Alamy Images:** Purestock. **38 Getty Images:** Jose Luis Pelaez Inc. (cr); Barbara Maurer (br); Yellow Dog Productions (bc). **40 Photolibrary:** Marcus Mok / Asia Images RM (bc). **43 Getty Images:** Bambu Productions (cl). **Mother & Baby Picture Library:** Ian Hooton (br, bl). **44 Getty Images:** First Light / Trevor Bonderud (br). **45 Getty Images:** Photographer's Choice / Lisa Valder. **46 Getty Images:** Martha Lazar (br). **47 Getty Images:** Ferguson & Katzman Photography / Halo Images (bl). **48 Getty Images:** Vanessa Berberian (br); LWA (cr); Robin Reeder / Reeder Studios, LLC (bc). **51 Getty Images:** Jens Lucking (bl). **54 Mother & Baby Picture Library:** Ian Hooton (cr). **56 Getty Images:** Andy Cox (br). **61 Corbis:** Markus Moellenberg (bl). **63 Getty Images:** Jamie Grill (bl); LWA (tl). **Mother & Baby Picture Library:** Ian Hooton (cb). **64 Corbis:** Lisa B. (cr). **66 Getty Images:** Jamie Grill (r). **67 Corbis:** Beth Dixson (cl). **71 Getty Images:** L. Ancheles (tr); Johner (tl). **72 Getty Images:** Photographer's Choice / Andersen Ross (bl). **73 Corbis:** David P. Hall (cb). **Getty Images:** Photographer's Choice / B2M Productions (bl). **Mother & Baby Picture Library:** Ian Hooton (tc). **74 Getty Images:** Jessica Boone (bc); Jamie Grill (br). **79 Getty Images:** Tom Morrison (tl); Dennis Novak (tc). **80-81 Corbis:** Gareth Brown. **83 Getty Images:** Joe Polillio (br). **84 Alamy Images:** Jacky Chapman (br). **Getty Images:** Doug Crouch (bc). **85 Alamy Images:** Picture Contact (br). **86 Getty Images:** Altrendo Images (bc). **Mother & Baby Picture Library:** Ian Hooton (cr). **87 Mother & Baby Picture Library:** Ian Hooton. **88 Getty Images:** Thomas Northcut (bl). **90 Getty Images:** Mimi Haddon (c); Sean Murphy (br). **93 Corbis:** Inspirestock. **96 Getty Images:** Stone / Jerome Tisne (cr). **97 Getty Images:** Iconica / Jamie Grill (cl); Stone / Eri Morita (bl). **98 Getty Images:** Lilly Dong (cr). **99 Getty Images:** Jamie Grill (bl). **103 Corbis:** RCWW, Inc. (cl). **Getty Images:** PhotoAlto / Sigrid Olsson (bl); Camille Tokerud (br). **104 Corbis:** Ghislain & Marie David de Lossy / Cultura. **105 Getty Images:** Andy Sacks (bl). **106-107 Getty Images:** Alexandra Grablewski. **108 Getty Images:** Jean Michel Foujols (bl). **109 Corbis:** Bernd Vogel (t). **110 Getty Images:** Hitoshi Nishimura (bc) (cr). **111 Getty Images:** Paul Viant (br). **112 Dorling Kindersley:** Julie Fisher (bc). **Mother & Baby Picture Library:** Paul Mitchell (cr). **114 Getty Images:** Derek Henthorn / STOCK4B (cr). **Mother & Baby Picture Library:** Ian Hooton (br). **115 Corbis:** Brooke Fasani (br). **Getty Images:** Bambu Productions (t). **117 Getty Images:** Altrendo Images (cl). **118 iStockphoto.com:** Iwona Rajszczak (cr). **119 Alamy Images:** Petr Bonek. **121 PunchStock:** Fuse (cl). **122 Getty Images:** Rosanne Olson (br). **124 Getty Images:** Altrendo Images (cr). **125 Photolibrary:** Folio Images (bl). **126 Getty Images:** Photolibrary (cr). **130 Getty Images:** Rich Reid (bc). **132 Getty Images:** Scott Hortop (br). **134 Corbis:** Kevin Dodge (br). **135 Mother & Baby Picture Library:** Ian Hooton. **136 Getty Images:** Ghislain & Marie David de Lossy (br). **138 Getty Images:** Ray Kachatorian (bc). **139 Alamy Images:** Enigma (bl). **Getty Images:** Kactus (cl). **141 Corbis:** Heide Benser (bl). **Getty Images:** Huntstock (cl). **142 Getty Images:** Andy Bullock (cr); Charles Gullung (br). **143 Photolibrary:** Arunas Klupsas. **144 Alamy Images:** Picture Partners (br). **147 Getty Images:** Robin Reeder / Reeder Studios, LLC (tl). **148 Getty Images:** Arthur Tilley (c). **149 Mother & Baby Picture Library. 151 iStockphoto.com:** John Prescott. **152 Alamy Images:** Manor Photography (bc). **155 Getty Images:** Ghislain & Marie David de Lossy (bl). **160 Getty Images:** Mimi Haddon (cr). **162 Mother & Baby Picture Library:** Ian Hooton (c). **168 Getty Images:** Richard Kolker (br). **Mother & Baby Picture Library:** Ian Hooton (bc, cr). **169 Getty Images:** Camille Tokerud. **170 Getty Images:** Milka Alanen (cr). **Mother & Baby Picture Library:** Ian Hooton (br). **SuperStock:** age fotostock (bc). **171 Corbis:** Etsa (cl). **172 Corbis:** Ariel Skelley (bl). **174 Alamy Images:** Sally Cooke (br). **Getty Images:** Peter Cade (cr); Images Of Our Lives (bc). **176 Getty Images:** Mel Curtis (bc). **178 Corbis:** Laurence Mouton / PhotoAlto (bc). **Getty Images:** Kactus (br). **179 Getty Images:** Natalie Kauffman (bl). **180 iStockphoto.com:** Jorge Salcedo (br). **182 Getty Images:** Jupiterimages (bc); David Oldfield (br). **183 Getty Images:** Photodisc (bc). **Mother & Baby Picture Library:** Ian Hooton (bl). **186 Getty Images:** Clarissa Leahy (bc). **187 Getty Images:** DK Stock / Garfield Hall (c).

All other images © Dorling Kindersley
For further information see: www.dkimages.com